Chasing Butterflies

Nathan Thompson

First Printing, 2020

ISBN 978-1-7347916-0-0

asdf Publishing
www.asdfPublishing.com

For Jasmine
You are my butterfly

Preface

The summer of 2007 I decided to embark upon an ill-advised adventure. My plan was to buy a motorcycle and take off on my own to see the country. I knew that I needed a decent amount of preparation if I was going to be successful. More than anything I needed money, a resource that I had balefully little of. I formulated a very simple plan: I would work my ass off all summer. I started pulling about sixty hours per week between two jobs with a goal of saving up five thousand dollars. I figured I could get a used bike for a grand, pick up the rest of the supplies I needed for about the same, maybe drop a few hundred on motorcycle lessons because I didn't want to break my neck just fifty feet from my house, and I'd still have a couple thousand for the trip itself. That would be more than enough for me to hit the road for a few months when the next summer rolled around.

As the season drew to a close, imagine my shock when I had actually come up with all the money. My bank account had five thousand and change, enough to get me through the next year while working around my school schedule, so I kept forwarding my plan. I learned to ride and found what seemed like a decent bike online. Trouble was, once the dust had settled and the title was in my name, the damn thing didn't run anymore. I'm not sure if it had to do with me putting it down on some ice just hours after I bought it, or if it was a lemon to begin with. I don't know because I didn't put any effort into diagnosing the problem. I let the bike rust away in a storage unit all winter and spring. When the next summer rolled around I watched my grand solo adventure pass me by.

So why am I telling you all this? Is that what this book is about? An obituary of my failed endeavors? Somewhat. It's more than that though. This is a book of stories. What does that mean exactly? Well, let me try to explain.

Throughout college I worked at the bowling alley on campus. I usually pulled the night shift because I had too many classes to work during the day. That meant I would typically be there from about 5:00 PM until sometime around midnight. I was working that shift one night of my freshman year when Eddie, Sheila, Logan, Darien, and I decided we'd go four-wheeling after we'd all clocked out. Why? Because we were dumb children with too much freedom. Somehow we thought that 12:30 AM on a moonless evening would be the ideal time to start clawing our way through terrain that placed heavy demands on our ability to see what was in front of us. In spite of the empirical stupidity of our decision, we had made it and by God we would follow through on it. So as midnight rolled around we closed up shop, stole about twelve Hershey bars from the candy stock so that we'd have s'mores materials, and hit the road.

Back in those days I was driving an Isuzu Trooper lovingly dubbed The Icebox, owing to the fact that it was a white box lacking any notion of aerodynamic design. I had taken it into the mountains with my coworkers once or twice before, so I wasn't too concerned about the physical toll on it. Still though, trying to navigate steep terrain, narrow gaps in trees, and ill placed rocks strewn about the path with nothing but the leader's headlights and a few handheld lanterns made for even slower going than usual. It wasn't until about 3:00 AM that we decided to make camp in a little clearing, and it wasn't until dawn broke a few hours later that we noticed the sign placed not twenty feet from us that read, quite plainly, "NO CAMPING."

Along with that sign, the early morning light revealed Eddie, Logan, and myself huddled around a fire pit collectively pondering what to make of the day. Being young men of a mountainous persuasion, we decided the best thing would be to venture out for a hike. We let Darien and Sheila continue their slumber as we wandered down the nearest path. It wound through the hills and, though it was getting late in the spring, we soon found an expansive slope covered in the remnants of that winter's snow. It was just off the trail to our left and we could have easily followed the well-worn path away from there, but dammit we had to conquer the slope to prove that we were undaunted by any conditions. Keep in mind though, this wasn't the soft, fluffy snow you'd find in January. No, this was the grizzled snow that had held on for months. The stuff with a rough crust on top that scraped up your ankles and grainy bits underneath that soaked through your shoes. The stuff that made you wish summer would get here already so that it would all melt away at last.

We began our conquest of the hill, but we quickly found that the incline was too steep to simply hike. We'd get maybe ten feet up the hundred foot slope then slide back down to the bottom. Fortunately though, we were carrying six knives between the three of us. We took one in each hand and began assaulting the slope, carving out footholds to support our weight, stabbing into the snow ahead of us to stabilize our ascent. It was tough work, and by the time we were halfway up the slope I was damn well ready to be done. That's likely why I got sloppy and began shifting my weight on a step before I had gotten enough purchase in my next knifehold. In that single moment everything gave way.

My foot scraped out of the hold, my knife sliced a deep gouge in the snow but didn't take, and I began sliding helplessly down the slope. I did my best to stab the snow as I slid, hoping desperately to be able to stop my descent, but it was to no avail. I slowed just enough to plan how to cushion myself when I hit the bottom, but there was nothing else I could do.

When I finally reached the base, I got up, dusted myself off, and realized the full effect of what had happened. By sliding all the way down the same trail I had gone up I had erased every single foothold I had carved for myself. I would have to start all over again. So that's what I did. This time I had the diligence to ensure I did everything right. Eventually, I arrived at the top of the slope, maybe ten minutes after Eddie and Logan, where we discovered we were actually near the summit of a very low peak. I could see it rising in front of us, but it was at such an angle that all I could see behind it was the sky. That couldn't be it though. We were in the Rocky Mountains after all, there had to be more beyond this peak. So I set out to find what there was.

The terrain up there was more conducive to hiking. It was angled such that it received direct sunlight most of the day, so the snow had pretty much all cleared. The only obstacles were small shrubs and low grass. Even so, Eddie and Logan were worn out from driving all night and fighting their way up the slope, so they decided to call it quits where we were. To be honest, I wanted to as well, but I had to know. I set out on my own, trudging up the last thousand feet until I finally reached the top. And what did I find once I got there?

Another mountain looming in the distance.

See, when we set out to climb a mountain, it doesn't really matter whether we succeed or fail. There's always another mountain after that one, and another after that, and another, and another. And every time we try to climb one we learn, we grow, and we come back with another story to tell.

So these are my stories. The stories of my triumphs and of my defeats. Of the road, and of my journey, and of my life.

Please enjoy.

1

December of 2006 brought one of the most hellacious blizzards of my lifetime to the Colorado front range. State records indicate the average depth was thirty-two inches in my hometown of Boulder. Streets were nearly impassable, even by foot. Entire cars disappeared in snowdrifts.

At the time, my first semester at the University of Colorado was drawing to a close. The only things standing between me and a well deserved break were my Calc II final and a nasty cold. The blizzard struck right in the middle of finals week and the whole university was in an uproar with rumors and misinformation. School had been officially canceled, final grades would stand as they were. No, the exams would be rescheduled after the break and spring semester would start a week late. Wrong, as long as the lights were on the campus was open. Not so, campus was closed but professors could still force students to take exams at the scheduled time, assuming they themselves could make it to campus at all.

I should rewind a bit. That morning, as the snow was just beginning to fall, I knew two things: I had to be in CHEM 140 that night at 7:30 to take the final or I was not passing that class, and the next day they were kicking all of us out of the dorms so that they could ensure thousands of 18-year-olds living on their own for the first time hadn't torn the buildings apart. I would be spending the following three weeks with my dad, and I sure as hell wasn't going to be waiting for a bus that may or may not show up that night once the blizzard was in full swing. In preparation for the university's mass exodus I brought my car up to The Hill and parked on the east side of 16th Street near campus so that I could walk the three blocks from the Chemistry building after my final and head straight to my dad's that night.

I spent the rest of the day back in my dorm, studying and trying to kick my illness. I had raided the on-campus store earlier in the week because I had about fifty bucks left from my meal plan that I needed to spend, so at least I had plenty of canned soup and the good fortune to be placed in a room with a working microwave. My neighbors across the hall had a microwave that would only turn on if the door was open. It was... disturbing. Eventually though the time came and I made my way over to CHEM 140 with the rest of my eighty person class. To my knowledge no one had heard an official announcement as to whether the final was happening, but none of us wanted to be the one that missed it and failed Calc II. The whole thing took me just about the full two and a half hours to complete, which meant I was back at The Icebox somewhere around 10:00 PM that night.

Now please allow me to explain the particular geography of the area as it will prove relevant shortly. Boulder is nestled in a valley at the base of the eastern foothills of the Rocky Mountains. The University of Colorado is located close to the western edge of town in an area residents refer to as The Hill. As such, the surrounding area and even the campus itself has a distinct downward slope from west to east. Now, remember how I said I parked on a street near the campus? And how I said I parked on the east side of the street? And how I said we were on course to accumulate thirty-two inches of snow during that blizzard?

When I arrived at my car, I discovered it was fairly well sunk in the snow. The drifts were most of the way up the tire and beginning to touch the bottom edge of the doors. I wasn't too concerned about it, I had forded rivers deeper than that in the past, but I was concerned that the tailpipe might be buried. I had heard stories that if a car's exhaust pipe was clogged, for instance if someone maliciously stuffed a potato in there, that the car would be thoroughly destroyed when it started up. Hoping to avoid that fate, I inspected the area behind The Icebox. Sure enough the snow had piled around that as well. I dug out enough of the snow to expose the exhaust, brushed the snow from the side of my car so that it didn't drift in when I opened the door, and finally made a paltry effort to dig around the rest of the car. At that point I was pretty confident that I could get out with only a little trouble, so I climbed in and started her up.

I can't remember exactly how The Icebox sounded, but at the time I knew that it sure didn't sound right. So I left the engine idling and inspected the outside of the car. There was still a little snow in the exhaust pipe, which I found weird. I figured it was just some light fluff that would have been blown out when the engine started. Maybe I was wrong though, maybe it needed a little help clearing out. So I bent down and tried to remove the block with my finger.

I'm not sure how fast that snowball exited the exhaust pipe. All I know is that one moment it was in there and the next my face was covered in ice and I was on my ass. It felt like I'd gotten into a snowball fight with a major league pitcher. At least The Icebox sounded a lot better, so I climbed back in and tried to make my way out. That's when I discovered that driving uphill after being buried in a snowdrift was not an easy feat. To make matters worse there were other cars around me, so I couldn't simply drift forward along the curb until I found someplace with more purchase to pull away. Instead, I had the idea that if I could compact the snow around my car enough I may be able to work my way out. So for the next forty-five minutes I patiently pulled forward and backward, forward and backward, swinging slightly further toward the center of the road before sliding back into the gutter. I nearly had it too, until at last I hit a patch of ice and slid so close to another car that I couldn't move without risk of taking out his bumper. It was time to throw in the towel. I called a friend to come out tow me away from the curb.

Now, I included this whole inane story because it's important to understand one thing: that was the first and only time that The Icebox let me down. I loved that car. It saw me through monsoons and blizzards, through midnight burger runs with ten of my closest friends packed into five seats, and through countless ventures into the mountains. It plodded along patiently as I learned to drive a manual, and it idled softly while we listened to the radio under the stars. That car was all a boy could ask for and it wasn't long before it had the chance to make it up to me. Four months after our state was shut down by the aforementioned blizzard I found myself in the driver's seat of The Icebox as part of a lean but eager convoy on an expedition to Utah for spring break.

It's generally agreed by all establishments of higher education across the nation that March is the proper month to unleash all students upon the unsuspecting world for a week of revelry in between months of study. Of course, in the absence of any official holiday during the season, every university makes their own decision as to when this break should fall. That year CU's break would be March 24th through April 1st. That worked well for Sterling, Alyson, Mikko, Tilly, and I, but we had one more member of our merry band. Flynn's break was the week before and only overlapped with ours by a weekend. Fortunately he was up for missing a few days of his education to extend the road trip with us, which was important as his presence was indispensable for the trip. To give us the most time possible together, we decided to head out as soon as everyone was done with classes on the 23rd, and return to Colorado on the 27th. After that, Flynn would make a hasty trip back to Minnesota to finish the semester.

In actuality, I spent very little of the 23rd in the classroom. The day before I was running errands with Mikko to prep for our journey. We were in charge of acquiring the necessary libations for the trip, which was a weighty task when all travelers were either eighteen or nineteen years old. We had a hookup though and had gathered pitch from everyone else in the group, so we just needed to put together a shopping list. It went as follows:

    90 Cans of terrible beer
    6 Assorted packs of decent beer
    1 Handle of cheap tequila
    1 Handle of cheap rum
    1 Fifth of cheap vodka

A sensible person would have done the math and realized that's 162 beers and 128 ounces of hard liquor. If the six of us drank five beers and four shots during each of the five nights in Utah then we'd be dead, but more importantly we'd still have alcohol left over. Mikko and I were not sensible people though, and our connection happily went to the store and came back with two hundred dollars worth of alcohol for our expedition.

The one major benefit of this wanton excess was that when it was evenly distributed in the back of The Icebox, it created a near-level surface eight inches deep across the entire trunk bed. We laid a few blankets on top and voilà! We had a false bottom to the SUV. Much easier to hide something when it's not a blatant bulge in one area of the trunk, especially since we were a bunch of minors transporting alcohol across state lines. From there we did actual packing, loading up tents, sleeping bags, and all necessary accessories. We headed over to Mikko's place and grabbed his tow-hitch mounted bike rack in case we wanted to do some riding in the canyons. It did block the rear door making it nearly impossible to access the trunk while the bikes were loaded, which was both a bad and good thing. The impediment kept prying eyes from opening it up and discovering our stash.

I bid Mikko farewell as the afternoon turned to evening on the 22nd. I had other things to attend to that night, but that's a story for another time. Suffice to say I wasn't headed back toward my dorm until just a little before sunrise. I left my car auspiciously off campus to keep it safe from any nosy police officers and finally made it to bed around 5:15 AM. At that point I'd already given up any hope of making it to my first three classes.

Annoyingly, it was impossible for me to ditch all my classes that day. If that hadn't been the case we might have been able to make the trip in a single day, but my last class was Calc III and I had already been struggling before one of the graders thoroughly screwed up my midterm the prior week. I had split an answer across multiple pages and he either misunderstood or just ignored half the work I'd done, resulting in a full drop in letter grade. That meant I had to go to class that afternoon to ask for a regrade from the professor. It would be about a month before I actually got a time slot to come in and plead my case, which turned out to be one of the most bizarre meetings of my college career.

But I digress. After I had finished at the university I headed over to my dad's because he insisted on doing a last minute check of The Icebox before I hit the open road. It was a little nerve wracking with the alcohol in the trunk. It was well camouflaged from anyone peering into the windows, but just opening the trunk would reveal our stash. He didn't discover any of that, but he did discover that my oil was so low it was nearly off the dipstick. I considered myself lucky on both counts. Earlier that year Nick had fused his entire engine while driving up the mountains because he hadn't changed the oil in his car for years. He'd ended up selling it for parts to the guy who towed him back to town. I was loathe to repeat that experience in the deserts of Utah.

With two fresh quarts of oil and a final reminder to drive safe, I left my dad's and made haste to Sterling's place. He was borrowing his sister's truck for the weekend and needed help from Mikko and I to get the camper top on it. It was an old family heirloom, one of those trucks that had seen the world twice over and was happy to still be humming. It took all three of us to lift the camper on the bed. In true brawn over brain fashion, we got the thing in place only to discover the bolts to keep it attached were all worn away. We made an emergency trip to the hardware store to buy what we needed and finally got the truck in order.

With that final chore done there was no longer a need for me to hang around. Tilly had arrived with a car full of groceries, so she and I piled everything into The Icebox and waved our goodbyes to Mikko and Sterling. The two of them would await the arrival of Flynn and Alyson so that they could all convoy together. In the meantime Tilly and I would get a head start and make sure we could secure a room at the hotel in Grand Junction.

It felt good to be out on the open road. The Icebox even performed pretty well during our first stretch along CO-93 as we wove our way south to I-70. We made good time to the outskirts of Eldorado, but all the miscellaneous trips that morning had meant I was getting a little low on gas. We pulled off to fill up and gather sustenance for the trip ahead. We had somehow neglected our imminent snacking needs when doing the main grocery shopping and only picked up food to be consumed around the campfire. The gas station had the usual assortment, so we grabbed chips and Gatorades. I finally confided in Tilly that I'd only had five hours of sleep the night before, so she insisted I get a couple Australian energy drinks that she knew from her native land. We also mutually agreed that we would need the latest issue of *Cosmo* for our camping adventure. Why a *Cosmo*? To this day I can't rightly answer that question except to say it was nothing new for our friends. In all the countless hours we'd spent together throughout high school, we'd somehow developed an affinity for lounging about and reading ridiculous articles to one another, men and women alike. I guess the takeaway is that it really doesn't matter what I did back then as long as I did it with the people that made me happy.

So, *Cosmo* in hand, we hit the road. I would soon come to learn that, of all the folks on the trip, Tilly was without question the best person to have as a passenger in my car. I'll shortly get to Sterling's experience driving Mikko across Colorado, and while I'm sure Alyson and Flynn had a pleasant time, Tilly was in tune to my needs almost to a fault. She was constantly asking if I needed more chips or more Gatorade or anything else. Looking back, Tilly was always one of the shepherds of our group. Someone who tended to us and kept us whole. I was really lucky to have her along for the ride, and I'm not just talking about the drive to Utah.

It was much appreciated too as I needed help keeping a calm nerve. As soon as we hit I-70 it was clear this trip was going to push The Icebox to its limit. We were lugging on every uphill stretch. Downshifting to fourth would give us barely enough juice to make the crest at speed, and dropping down to third would nearly redline the engine altogether. Each attempt to pass another vehicle was a harrowing experience. I had to build speed going downhill and pray I had enough runway to make it past before we started to climb again. I successfully pulled this maneuver a few times, but at least once a semi I was overtaking decided to build some speed on the downhill as well, leaving me without enough space to make the cut back when the uphill portion rose ahead of us. When that happened I had to do everything possible to eek out enough speed just to keep pace with the semi. Sometimes I'd begin slipping back, much to the chagrin of the motorists behind me. I got more than a few high beam flashes and horn honks as we were getting started on our journey.

The whole drive toward the Continental Divide was much the same story. Muscling our way as best we could through the ups and recovering lost time during the downs. At least we started devouring the miles when we finally reached the Western Slope. I punched the gas as hard as I could on the downhills and managed to hit about ninety-three mph a couple times in between brief uphill stints. I was keeping an eye on the speedometer to see how close I could get to a hundred as I had yet to ever drive that fast in a car. Once the terrain leveled out I resigned myself to more reasonable speeds. Before long we were passing Rifle and Palisade, and finally we arrived at Grand Junction.

The plan was to get a hotel that night then make the final drive to Vader Rock the next morning so we could make camp in daylight. Sterling had given us precise directions to the hotel / restaurant / gas station where we would stay as per his family tradition. Tilly and I went in and booked a room for four figuring that would guarantee us two queen beds and enough floor space to sleep all six of us comfortably. We then headed up and watched TV while waiting for the rest of our crew to catch up. The other two cars pulled up about a half hour later with quite a grand entrance. Mikko had been hotboxing Sterling's truck for the entire five hour trip, and when they opened the doors in the parking lot a vast cloud of smoke announced their arrival. Both of them were blitzed even though Sterling himself hadn't hit the pipe once. Naturally, he was glad to be off the road at last.

From there we decided that our top priority was to get dinner. The four men piled into Flynn's car to find a place that was still open at 11:00 PM in Grand Junction while Tilly and Alyson made themselves at home in the hotel. We came across a Burger King, and under much duress we decided it was the best option. We pulled into the drive through only to realize we had somehow oriented ourselves in the direction opposite the intended flow of traffic. Rather than waste time trying to turn around, someone suggested we just go through backwards. In our road-weary state that seemed like a good idea, so we pulled up to the speaker and Sterling ordered from the front passenger seat. We got it all settled and then Flynn, guided by our masterful skills, reversed the entire way around a corner up to the window. The usual grunt laborer at the register didn't seem to care, but his manager, a bear of a woman, shoved him aside and leaned out the window for maximum screaming efficiency as she exclaimed, "This is unacceptable! Drive-thrus do not work this way!!" So we made the car behind us wait while we turned around to receive our food.

Upon our return to the hotel, Mikko demanded access to my car so that he could grab a beer. I had put forth the proposal that no alcohol would be consumed that night. My argument was, why take the risk? Mikko and Sterling were already lit, and if we got caught with the booze and other substances then so much for our spring break trip. In response, Mikko went off about how there weren't supposed to be any parents on the trip and we should be allowed to do whatever the fuck we want, so to shut him up I tossed him the keys and told him to make sure everything was hidden when he was done. He returned with a few bottles and assured me that everything was well hidden. Everyone had a beer, finished our meal, and settled in for the night.

The next morning we made our way to Otto's, the little diner that adjoined the hotel, to fill our bellies for the day to come. The host sat the six of us at a deceptively small booth next to the kitchen. Walking up to it I thought it would have no issue fitting everyone, but then we spent the morning elbowing each other in the ribs as we tried to shovel food into our mouths. It seemed the staff were just as burdened by the little space as we were because shortly after we sat down we saw an old man peer intently at us through the kitchen door, or more accurately peer intently at Mikko through the kitchen door, before he receded while audibly muttering, "I never get any help." We glanced at each other and suppressed mutual, empathetic chuckles.

Breakfast was pretty good in spite of the cramped quarters. Alyson and Sterling each had a bagel, Flynn and I had the breakfast burrito, Tilly got the french toast, and Mikko got the huevos rancheros. No one thought to suggest that gas station huevos would not be the best accompaniment for another five hours in the car. Thus Mikko would spend the drive fouling the air in Sterling's cab even worse than the day before.

With our appetite sated we packed up our gear and headed out. We got a brief awkward glance from a cleaning lady as the six of us piled out of the four person room all at once, but we didn't pay her any mind as we made our way to the cars. It was at that time that I finally learned what Mikko had meant when he assured me the beer was well hidden. He had pulled one case into the front seat, pulled out the bottles he would bring to the room, then tugged a blanket over part of it. If one were to examine the interior of the car from the passenger side window, one would see a cube shaped blanket. From the driver's side, one could read quite clearly the bold face letters "BLUE MOON BEER CO" printed across the box that was lovingly tucked in with a blanket.

Granted, I was and am belaboring the point, but the draconian Minor In Possession laws were a serious concern for a group of baby faced college freshmen such as ourselves. Traveling to an utterly foreign land only heightened my sensitivity on the subject. Once I had properly repacked the car I laid into Mikko for his carelessness. He just laughed, and after a moment I couldn't help but join him. That was one thing about Mikko, he had an exuberance that won everyone over. After all, we were just a bunch of college kids out for a rowdy spring break of camping and drinking. Nothing new under the sun. It was time for me to relax and enjoy the trip.

With all our belongings once again packed we headed to the gas station for a quick fill up then hit the road once again. Flynn was in the lead, next was Sterling, and I was picking up the rear. Just about the time we merged onto I-70, Tilly and I noticed something fly off of Sterling's car. At first we thought he had thrown something out the window, but as we passed by we realized it was his gas cap. I hit the brakes as fast as I could and pulled off. Sterling was none the wiser, so I frantically tried to radio him while Tilly ran back to retrieve it. I managed to get ahold of the other cars and tell them to pull off before they got out of range, then I looked back to discover Tilly was already about two hundred feet up the highway. I didn't realize I had gone so far past the cap, so I threw The Icebox into reverse and did about twenty mph the wrong way along the shoulder to pick her up because I'm a goddamn gentleman. Luckily the gas cap was undamaged, so she climbed back in and we drove up to meet Sterling. After I presented him the cap he kindly asked if we had also found Flynn's.

I stared at him dumbfounded. How did this happen to *both* cars at once? In any case, we had not found Flynn's gas cap, so Sterling and I made a quick turn through an emergency vehicle loop while the law abiding Flynn drove a few miles up the road to the next town with a proper turnaround. He arrived back at the gas station a few minutes after us and together we found his cap thrown to one side of the parking lot. We set off for the second time that morning with all cars finally intact.

The next two hours were rather uneventful. We stopped in Green River because it was the last gas station we would see for the next four days. Soon we were off I-70 and heading down country roads to the heart of Utah. There were stretches of land where the road carried on straight ahead of us as far as the eye could see. I thought about the drive the day before, getting The Icebox almost to the one hundred mph threshold, and it made me want to gun it down the straightaway again. I abstained though after I decided it was unwise to pass the only guy that knew where we were going.

Eventually we found our way onto the dirt road leading to our campsite. We passed by a few other campers along the route, but they tapered off as we made our way deeper into the

Goblin Valley region. The last leg of our trip required us to do some proper four-wheeling through a dry creek bed. All of the fine silt had eroded away leaving only a trail of one- to two-hundred pound rocks that we had to drive across, bobbing frequently as we tried unsuccessfully to find a level path. Sterling was the first through and then he guided Flynn and I along the way. I had managed to bash the bike rack a couple of times coming off some of the larger rocks, but at last we arrived.

Vader Rock.

Aptly named for its ominous appearance at night. Looking at it from base camp it was roughly a 500-foot sheer rock face that provided the boundary between two canyons. Alyson and Tilly worked to rebuild the worn down fire pit and stack a few rocks to form a makeshift table. Somehow in our haste we had only managed to pack one folding table, and we would need more workspace to properly make camp. Meanwhile the four of us boys went off to gather firewood. Strictly speaking, it wasn't necessary for all of us to gather firewood, but for my own part I intended to take every possible chance to learn from Sterling. This was the first trip I'd ever been on that was arranged by someone my age, and in truth I was pretty awestruck that Sterling could organize and lead us to the canyons of Utah without breaking a sweat.

The four of us ventured into the hillsides looking for suitable trees. The slopes around us were littered with cedars, but Sterling urged us to find pinion pines instead. We spent maybe twenty minutes scouting about, all the while pestering Sterling with questions of why we couldn't just take down a cedar. Eventually he handed over his ax, which happened to be the only ax anyone thought to bring, and Mikko and I took turns swinging at the nearest tree. We quickly found that the cedars had a very shallow outer bark that could be cut in a single swing. That gave a false hope that it could actually be felled with an ax. We just as quickly learned that the cedars had a rock solid core that was impossible to cut through. We spent about five minutes swinging the ax before finally giving up. By that time Flynn and Sterling had also given up all hope of finding any pinion. It would seem Sterling had cleared the hillside of that species during family trips long before, so we had no other option than to bring down the cedar. Since the ax was no help we took turns standing above a cedar lobbing 30-pound rocks at the trunk until it finally uprooted. Once it was down we hauled the shattered branches back to the campsite.

The afternoon was getting late, so we decided to put off any more firewood gathering for the next day. We set up a ring of collapsible chairs around the fire pit and I found a nice spot to hang my hammock. As night crept up we built a meager fire and roasted marshmallows. We started circulating some tortilla chips with cheese sauce and cracked open some beers to wash it down. At some point Tilly leaned over to Alyson and bopped the mouth of Alyson's beer bottle with the butt of her own. For those that don't know the trick, doing so caused an explosion of carbon dioxide from the beer, causing most of it to spill across the ground. Tilly had a good laugh, but Mikko, Flynn, Sterling, and I unanimously declared that wasting beer in the name of humor was unacceptable in the court of manliness. It was therefore declared that Tilly's honorary testicles were to be unceremoniously revoked. Tilly played along and demanded to know how she could earn her testicles back, which was a great way to put four adolescent men completely off balance.

After a quick conference on the matter, it was decided to establish Man Points as a form of currency. Tilly, as with all of us from that point forward, could gain or lose them based on the actions we took. We further decided that the first step on Tilly's journey to reclaim her testicles would be to eat a nacho on which a mosquito had landed and died. Tilly didn't even blink an eye. We were in for a good trip.

Grumblings arose when the tortilla chips ran out, but hard feelings were put aside as we gazed into the fire. Flynn had brought some sealed packs of tuna and clams and proceeded to whip up a seafood pesto to serve over spaghetti. A hearty meal like that raised everyone's spirit. Someone packed a bowl and began circulating it. Mikko and I each began to play with sticks, shoving them into the coals, then removing them and watching the weak flames at their tips putter out in the night air. A weak debate broke out between us on a subject only the rocks remember now. I gave that up for the simple pleasures of lighting my Zippo off the flame of the stick. Meanwhile Mikko, who by then had consumed a couple beers and a couple bowls, decided to enjoy the simple pleasure of taking his fire-hardened stick, still red hot at the tip, and stabbing me square in my hand. I cussed him out, but he was too far gone to care. The group awarded me three Man Points as consolation, and I settled myself to nursing my injury in a bucket of dish water. The burning stab wound was small, but it still blistered for the next four days. Sometimes Mikko's exuberance was not so charming.

Eventually we each made our own way to our separate abodes. Sterling climbed into the camper on his truck while Flynn and Alyson each had a tent to themselves. Mikko and Tilly pitched a tent for themselves a few hundred feet away from the rest of the group. For my own part, I emptied the back of the The Icebox and folded up the seats. That gave me the perfect amount of space to lie down as long as I wedged myself diagonally across the floor. It was enough for a decent night's sleep.

In the morning Sterling made a quick but filling breakfast of pancakes then we were off for a hike. Since the creek bed posed a very annoying obstacle to entering and exiting the campsite we condensed down to two cars. Alyson, Tilly, and I piled into Flynn's car while Mikko and Sterling continued to drive point in Sterling's truck. That gave the four of us the opportunity to stare exasperated at Mikko as he climbed out the window to sit on the door itself. He contentedly bobbed along in the open air as Sterling gassed the truck to an even sixty mph through the dirt roads.

Eventually we got to the trail and discovered close to a dozen families milling around the trailhead, some just arriving and some just setting off along the same path we would travel. One family had even brought their pet chihuahua along for the trek. That put a damper on my expectation of a fearsome adventure to be had, but we set off nonetheless into a canyon that Sterling had selected especially for us.

Mikko's excitement hadn't abated at all. As we approached the mouth of a canyon he began literally bouncing off the walls. At one point he charged up a thirty-foot rock incline and turned to sprint all the way back down at twice the speed. Flynn and I conferred in that moment and decided that if he hurt himself it was minus two Man Points for needless exuberance resulting in injury. Mikko's descent was relatively controlled until he hit the sandy trail bed with an awkward footing, stumbled headfirst toward the opposing canyon wall, and caught himself just short of bashing his face on a rock. He was a bit more subdued after that.

As we ventured forth the canyon walls steadily became steeper and tighter until we were thoroughly boxed in. If we looked straight up we could see the sky above us, but it was fairly well obstructed by thirty feet of sheer rock face on either side of our path. As Utah was still experiencing the mild temperatures of spring, and the sunlight was hard pressed to reach the canyon floor, we quickly encountered pools of standing water stretched across the width of the trail. Most were easy enough to pass if we braced ourselves on either wall of the canyon and shimmied above the surface of the water. Eventually though we came upon a pool that was too wide to span. Mikko, Tilly, and Alyson had the foresight to wear clothes that would easily dry, so they waded through without much heed to the water. Flynn, Sterling, and I were all wearing jeans and didn't have the same luxury. We opted instead to strip down to our boxers and throw our clothes in our bags so we wouldn't be forced to spend the remaining hike chafing ourselves on wet denim.

All was fine until, just as we had exited the pool, we heard the voices of many children coming from ahead of us. We each made a mental calculation of how fast those voices were approaching and, to a man, came to the conclusion that it was impossible to get dressed in time. Instead, the three of us stood there holding our packs in front of our waists to give us more than just a thin sheet of water-logged cotton separating us from the five kids, all under ten years old, all with parents in tow, that had to shuffle past us on their way through the canyon. Once they were past we all dressed as quickly as we could, which would have been an easier task if we weren't all laughing hysterically at the absurdity of what had just transpired, and then we got the hell out of there.

Once we were out of the canyon, Sterling announced to the group that we were about halfway done with the loop. The remaining three or four miles would be gorgeous albeit not very noteworthy for this story. There was a lingering mystery that would plague the rest of our hike though. Shortly after we emerged from the canyon we discovered a sizable blood splatter on one of the rocks. Like, if Mikko hadn't caught himself and instead had gone face first into the canyon wall, he would have created something like this. Whoever had left the blood spatter had since vacated the area, yet for the rest of the hike we would see more droplets of dried blood along the trail. They seemed to mark every permanent surface. We may walk a few hundred feet through shifting sands without a sight of them, but as soon as there was a boulder to scramble over we were sure to find another few drops. How did someone presumably bash his head open and then continue through the second half of the loop? This became the singular topic of conversation within our group. We half expected to find an incapacitated body waiting for us around every corner.

Ultimately, we found no such thing. As we returned to the parking lot where we had begun our trek there were still no injured persons to be found. Later that night Sterling would comment on how disappointed he was with our outcome. He was hoping to have one final, Scooby-Doo style reveal in which we unmasked the maligned party and solved the mystery once and for all. Some secrets the desert keeps for herself though. With nothing left to do, we threw our packs in the cars and headed off.

We made a quick stop at a ranger's station on the way to our campsite to refill our depleted water stores. We had a five gallon canteen from Sterling and a three gallon one from Flynn. Mikko's folks had lent another three gallon canteen for the cause, but they had been unable to find the little plastic cap to seal it when not in use. In lieu of that, we had covered the mouth with a plastic bag, thinking that would hold. We filled all of the aforementioned containers and hit the road.

After we were well out of sight of the station, Mikko climbed out of his window to once again ride the dirt roads dangling out of Sterling's truck. At this point Tilly and I figured it must be safe enough since Mikko hadn't died yet, so we did the same in Flynn's car. Pretty soon we were both commenting that the air was very humid for the desert. But, no, it wasn't humid, it felt like it was raining. Raining out of a clear sky? That couldn't be right either, but we were definitely being hit in the face with droplets of water.

Finally we realized what was going on. I yelled through the window at Flynn, and he radioed Sterling to tell him water was pouring out of his truck bed. Sterling pulled to a stop and opened the camper hatch to find Mikko's canteen had fallen over, torn through the thin plastic film, and released nearly a gallon of water over his pack and whatever other belongings were back there. He heaved the canteen out of the truck bed and emptied it with as much rage as he could imbue upon the act. Of course, pouring water out of a spout is a rather benign proceeding no matter how it's done, so by the end he was simply letting the water drain in a crestfallen manner. He tossed the empty canteen back in the truck and we set off again toward camp.

Being that it was a Sunday, most of the other folks near our site had decided to break camp and head home, which worked out perfectly for us. Rather than spending another evening smashing rocks against cedars we raided the vacated camps for any leftover firewood. We found a few big logs that Sterling was able to smash with the sledgehammer side of his ax head and we were set for the night. We ate dinner, cooked s'mores, and started passing a pipe around the group, which would soon lead to one of the most terrifying moments of Sterling's life.

I had decided to refrain from smoking. Instead I sat back and laughed along as the topic of conversation became more and more nonsensical. At one point though, as I was amusing myself with a hand spade we'd brought for dousing the fire, Sterling threw an insult my way that I couldn't let slide. I gave him a quick jab in the gut as retribution, not meaning to really hurt him, but he immediately froze. The expression on his face conveyed more terror than I had ever seen in my life. I cautiously asked what was wrong, to which he exclaimed, "I thought you killed me!" To Sterling's credit, throughout the trip I had been playing with a butterfly knife, practicing ways to flick it open and closed with as much flare as possible. So when Sterling saw me stab him with something metallic in my hand, he honestly believed I had just run him through with a knife. All this he explained breathlessly as his brain slowly reoriented itself to a reality in which he was not about to bleed to death in the desert sands. Everyone else thought it was hilarious and conversation continued.

We kept our vigil around the fire for another few hours while we discussed many ridiculous things. Finally though it was time to retire. Just before we put out the fire, Alyson drew our attention to a large, iridescent ring that hung in the sky around the moon. Sterling explained that it was a Moon Dog, and the prevailing wisdom was that the larger the Moon Dog, the colder the night would be. He then proclaimed that it was probably the largest one he'd ever seen. With that we went our separate ways to weather the night ahead.

One by one we awoke the next morning and began preparing another breakfast of pancakes to sate us for the day ahead. Mikko and Tilly were the last to rise. The flap on the front of their tent hung open due to a broken zipper, which prompted the rest of us to try lobbing pebbles through the door to rouse them. We were all terrible shots and didn't land anything in the tent, but they woke up nonetheless and assured us they would soon be out. We wanted to make sure everyone got a hearty breakfast in preparation for the events ahead. That would be the day that we summited Vader Rock.

Sterling outlined the journey a bit over breakfast. We would start by scrambling up a small boulder field to reach the top of the canyon that flanked Vader Rock to the north. Then, to his recollection, it was a relatively mild hike up to the summit. Tilly had been dealing with severe knee issues for sometime, so she was a little apprehensive but decided to make a go of it. We packed up some water and headed off.

After about seventy-five vertical feet Tilly decided it was too much for her knee, so she turned back for the camp. Alyson accompanied her so she wouldn't have to spend all morning alone. Sterling, Flynn, Mikko, and I pressed onward and soon made it out of the canyon. There we stopped for a short break in the shade of a boulder to take in our surroundings. I learned a sobering lesson about the instability of the landscape when I accidentally kicked a two-foot rock off its resting point. It gained momentum and rolled most of the way down the slope before bouncing off a ledge and entering a state of free fall. Sterling had seen a family of bikers heading down a trail that intercepted the rock's path, so he jumped up and shouted "Freedom!" as loud as he could. The bikers got the message and stopped to watch the rock's final plummet and subsequent explosion as it hit the ground more than a hundred feet below where it had dislodged. The family decided with us up top is was probably safest to turn back the way they came.

We continued our ascent, but somehow we were unable to find the mild hike Sterling had promised us. Instead we progressed in fits and starts as the route was segmented into tiers. We would spend a few minutes assessing the options before us, set about a maneuver that would get us another twenty or thirty feet closer to the summit, and then repeat the process. At least the scenery was beautiful. Periodically we would find little windswept caves along the walls, and we would duck inside for a minute and talk about how awesome it would be to spend the night on one of the precipices. Then we would set off again. Nothing was so technical that we needed climbing equipment, but all of it required a certain degree of planning and careful execution.

The first maneuver once we had reached Vader Rock proper was to squeeze our way up a crevasse. Flynn beat around the base of it with a stick because it was just the sort of cool, dark place a rattler would love to nap in. When nothing emerged we made our way up. The handholds and footholds were fine for climbing, it was just a bit of a squeeze getting our day packs through the very top. Next was a slope that was a little too steep to ascend standing up, so we lumbered forward on all fours. I got a little careless just as we were reaching the top of that section and tried to use an unstable rock as a handhold. It came loose and slid down the slope, rolling over my ankle in the process. It wasn't bad enough to bruise, but it was another wake up call to stay alert.

Beyond that there were numerous patches where we had to scramble backward on all fours just to give us added stability. Being as I am deathly afraid of heights, I was none too happy for some of those sections. I particularly disliked the portions where I was already maneuvering backward on all fours before coming to an outcropping that was a foot or two high. Something about hoisting myself up on poor footing made me especially upset. Since the entirety of Vader Rock was a sort of sandstone we all repeatedly experienced the shock of hand holds snapping off under our grasp. We took to ascending one at a time, carefully retracing the path of the person ahead of us, assuming that it must be safe to traverse. This worked well for the most part until the final section before the summit.

As I neared the crest, a foothold that both Mikko and Flynn had used before me popped off. It wasn't a small piece either, it was a sizable chunk that broke again into two foot-long pieces on the way down the slope. I had too much weight on it when it came loose so I went sliding down after it almost all the way to the previous tier. Sterling had been behind me for that maneuver and had the good sense to get out of the way as I slowed to a halt. He pushed the rocks further down the slope while I dusted myself off, then he told me to go for it again. I did, and I silently cursed him and everyone else all the way up. Why had I let them talk me into this? Why didn't I turn back with Tilly and Alyson? I hated heights. I hated that stupid sandstone. I hated everything about--

My God. Look at that view.

We had hauled ourselves up about five hundred feet in the heart of God's Country, as Sterling so often called it. I could not have begun to imagine what awaited me at the end of the climb. The land stretched for countless miles in all directions until the earth finally curved out of sight. I stood staring for a good three minutes at a mass of clouds brewing on the edge of the world. All of us were awestruck.

We soon decided to venture toward the eastern side of Vader Rock so we could look down on the campsite. However, we discovered the landing where we had summited didn't connect to that edge. There was maybe a fifteen foot gap between us and a vantage point where we'd be able to see our tents. We dropped back down to the previous tier and scouted a path that ran under an overhang from the landing above. Mikko was taking point and stepped across a series of boulders while supporting himself with the overhang above. It was a good thing too, because he caught himself on that overhang when one of the massive rocks gave way under his foot and slid down the crevasse below. He shot us a look that said his heart rate had just about doubled, then continued undeterred. We followed in his footsteps without incident.

A quick jump over a gap and we were ready to climb the final height to the easternmost summit. Flynn and Mikko scouted the climb and each found their own route on either side of the rock face. Once the two of them were clear I began up the path that Flynn had taken and Sterling made his way around to the other side to follow Mikko. I grabbed what I thought was a good handhold, but as it gave way I dropped my weight back down. I must have made a commotion because Sterling shouted a tentative, "You good?" in a voice that seemed to imply he was really asking, "Are you still alive?" I assured him I was. He offered the possibility that his route may be a bit easier, but I was already committed and soon joined the rest of the group at the top.

At last we had made it to the outcropping we had seen from our camp below. We looked over the edge and saw Tilly and Alyson tanning on blankets near the campfire. We shoved a few rocks off the back side of the outcropping to draw their attention, and listened to the dull thud as they first impacted the ground, and then the massive gunshot that came back as the sound echoed off the far canyon wall. The ladies looked up, saw us, and gave great, masculine shouts to celebrate our prowess. Sterling responded with this jewel of a limerick:

> There once was a man in the grass,
> Whose balls were made out of brass.
> When they banged together,
> They made stormy weather,
> And lightning shot out of his ass!

He paused at each line so we could hear it echo back to us. Try as I might to deny it, that limerick is forever ingrained upon my mind. Maybe it's because that's the first limerick I had ever heard in its entirety, and the novelty of it stuck with me. More likely it's because my brain was trying to drink in every single detail of that experience as I was peering out on the vast world beneath my feet. We saw what appeared to be a lone mountain rising from the landscape an immeasurable distance to the southeast. There was blue sky all around the formation, but tumultuous clouds billowed directly over it. Flynn, Mikko, and I wondered aloud why there was such a singular mountain, but Sterling assured us it was merely a trick of the distance. We were in fact looking at a range of mountains, though if I were to hold my hand at arm's length I could blot it out with just my palm.

While we sat there and drank in the beauty of the landscape Mikko packed a bowl. It wasn't until he completed the task that he realized he had forgotten a lighter. Flynn came to his aid, but even so Mikko was the only one that smoked up there. The rest of us agreed that it would be best to keep our full faculties for the climb down. We sat around for another twenty minutes then decided it was time to climb back down. We probably would have explored the summit for another hour or more if we had the option, but none of us had the forethought to pack a lunch, so the length of our stay was limited by our stomachs. Before we left, we gathered in a circle, locked arms, thrust our crotches three times toward the center while making masculine grunts, then broke the huddle to flex and shout, "Yeah!" That was the custom of the day for celebrating such manly accomplishments as surmounting a five-hundred-foot rock in the heart of Utah. With that done we began our descent.

At that point Sterling repeated his claim that there was an easy way up Vader Rock. All the scrambling we did was really a quick substitute so we wouldn't waste time looking for it. Now that we had started a new leg of our journey we took him at his word and decided to waste time looking for it. We made our way back to the first summit area and began examining the canyon on the south side of the rock. It didn't look at all promising, but we decided if we had enough energy we may be able to hike around the top of that canyon and climb down the wall opposite us.

We decided to stick close to the south canyon in case an opportune path presented itself while we made our way toward our initial climb. At one point we discovered a channel that had been carved by runoff water over the course of a few centuries, so we decided to see where it led. We trekked along it for a bit, and just before it let out into the south canyon we came upon a six-foot drop. Mikko was just about to leap down when I posed the question, would we be able to make it up again if we had to come back this way? After a quick huddle we decided to send Mikko to scout the route and tell us what he found. He hopped down, walked to the edge, and delivered the following report that inspired oh so much confidence in us, "It's doable, it's just... a cliff..."

Goddammit Mikko.

After a bit more discussion it was decided that we'd probably be able to make that first section, but then what? We had no idea what other hairy parts were in store for us afterward, and there was a good chance we would get rimmed up in the canyon. It just wasn't plausible. Sterling helped Mikko climb back up and we continued on.

Finally we reached the end of the road: a rock ledge on the southern end of Vader Rock. We examined the prospect of continuing around to the far rim of the south canyon, but it didn't seem like we would be in any better shape heading that way. It would've been at least another three mile hike and who knows what we would find when we arrived. We decided to try one last excursion a little further west. If we didn't find anything promising that way then we would head toward the path we originally took up.

As luck would have it, Sterling recognized the path he had found years before when he first climbed Vader Rock. It was another natural spillway carved down through the rock. To get to it, we took turns lowering the person ahead of us down a five-foot drop that had been worn smooth of any handholds. Somehow I ended up in the back of the procession and had to slide down while Sterling and Flynn spotted me. It was more unnerving than I would have liked as the path we landed on was less than three feet wide, and just beyond it was about an eight-foot drop that I had no intention of tumbling down. Fortunately, Flynn and Sterling ensured that didn't happen.

We followed that path until we arrived at a point that all of us recognized. We had examined it when we were first searching for a way up and decided it was doable but insanely difficult. It didn't look much better on the other side. Directly ahead of us was a ten-foot drop into about a two-foot deep pool. If we had waited a hundred years it would've probably eroded to a depth that we could safely jump down into, but we didn't have that kind of time. To our right, fifteen feet up, was a one-foot wide ledge that had connected to our path ten yards back and went to a ridge up out of sight. To our left was a four-foot tall, round ledge without any handholds that led to a gentle grade down to the next tier. A ways away we could see the landing where I'd nearly kicked that sizable rock onto those unsuspecting bikers below. How long ago was that? Regardless, we were just one maneuver away from done. One maneuver I couldn't do.

Mikko was in the lead and spent a long while dubiously eyeing the rock before calling Sterling to the front to examine the route. Sterling had the confidence that came with knowing he had done it before, and after contemplating prospective handholds for a minute, he half-scrambled, half-flung himself at the rock and worked his way to the top.

It was my turn next. I was still standing at the back of the group, but since I had the least confidence in my ability to make the maneuver Sterling declared I was not to be the last man up. I shimmied to the front of the line and stared at the rock. Then at the drop. Then at the rock. Then at the drop. All the while Sterling crouched above me with an outstretched hand. Once I started moving he would be the only anchor I had. I psyched myself up as best I could, warned Sterling to be ready because I was about to jump, tensed every muscle in my body, and then I didn't move. I didn't even take my hand off the rock to reach for Sterling. I was frozen. I couldn't go forward. I had to go back and find another path. Mikko and Flynn could probably have made it but they decided to come with me. Sterling had to stick with the path he chose though. He had cleared the hard part, and it would only be harder to come back from it. Thus the fellowship was broken.

Mikko, Flynn, and I worked our way back up to the ledge on our right, which was nerve-wracking enough for me but still better than the alternative. As soon as we had surmounted that wall we knew exactly where we were. We were at the first scramble we had come up. I noticed an awkwardly tilted rock and suddenly realized my ankle still hurt from when it rolled on me. Until then the pain had faded from my consciousness. Mikko and Flynn quickly sidled down the slope, but I was taking my time doing a little crab walk. Once the two of them reached the bottom they began searching for the crag that we'd climbed up at the proper start of our ascent. We all knew that it must be somewhere on this tier, but they were having trouble finding it. Just about the time I finished my descent, we heard Sterling calling us. He had found the crag we were looking for, but going down appeared to be a little more treacherous than coming up. We found another crack and used it to get down instead. After a few short maneuvers we were back on hiking ground.

Mikko and Flynn were eager to get back to camp, so they took off as fast as they could. I was following in their tracks, but I kept tripping over my own shoe laces that had somehow worked themselves into long tangles from all the scrambling. I finally stopped altogether and cut them down to a reasonable length. Then I noticed Sterling making his own way down. Evidently he had chosen a worse path than our companions and the going was slow. I made my way to him and we hiked down together.

Once we made it out of the canyon I stopped to ask Sterling how many vertical feet we had ascended. Even though we hadn't done any technical climbing I knew that summiting Vader Rock would be one of the accomplishments that would define my college years, and I was grasping for some sort of way to quantify it. He told me that he figured it was about five hundred feet, and I agreed with him. Then he pointed toward a single crack near the front of the rock face. He explained that the seemingly little gap we had jumped at the summit actually opened up into that crack. Some poor footwork up there would have meant we had roughly five hundred feet to contemplate whether or not we'd lived a full and meaningful life. At the time, he figured it was best to withhold that information from the rest of us. Looking back on how the prospect of a ten-foot drop froze me in my tracks, that was probably the right call.

At long last we arrived back in camp. Flynn had already set off in search of more firewood. Sterling and I grabbed a beer and mingled with Tilly and Alyson for a bit. Since none of us had a watch on the climb, it was only then that we found out our journey had taken us about four hours to complete. By then I was numb in body and mind, so I took off after Flynn to forage for firewood. Sterling took the opportunity to lounge around camp for a while as he was no longer responsible for leading a band of harebrained teenagers up a treacherous rock face with no technical equipment whatsoever. Mikko took three hits of acid, so he was in his own world. He spent the time mostly lying on rocks or in my hammock, occasionally proclaiming "huevos!" as Otto's World Famous Huevos Rancheros wreaked havoc on his bowels. It was a term that was adopted by the lot of us before the trip was done.

Flynn and I had given up on the ax, but we found an area rich with broken trunks and large branches. We started making a stockpile about one hundred feet from camp. After that had been built up a fair amount I hauled a load to the camp as Flynn continued to hunt. On my first return I enlisted Sterling to carry more of the stockpile. He made one trip, but after seeing the massive amount we were accumulating he decided to renovate the fire pit so that it could accommodate a larger fire. On my second trip back I found him pulling the floor stones out from under the ash. He called me over to show me how much thermal mass had accumulated in the fire pit the night before. He grabbed a water bottle and spritzed the stone that he'd just pulled out. Even though it had been nearly twelve hours since we extinguished the fire, half the water boiled into a dense cloud of steam as soon as it hit the stone. The other half continued to sizzle on the surface until it too evaporated in the desert air.

By then Flynn had started hauling wood to the campsite as well, so I left Sterling to toil in the fire pit under the desert sun. It took three more trips before we had retrieved all the fuel. Once we were done I decided it was time to sit down and have myself a rest. Flynn on the other hand, went straight into breaking the logs as most of them were too large to fit into the fire pit. Plus one Man Point.

At this point Mikko was thoroughly feeling the acid and decided the best course of action was to take a walk. We all watched him go, wondering if we should stop him given his current state. Sterling was the only one ambivalent to the situation. He continued his work in the fire pit and reminded us that from the very outset he had said that he wouldn't babysit anyone on their drug trips. Since no one else wanted to take on that responsibility either we reluctantly turned our backs on Mikko as he made his way into the desert. Tilly was the most distraught by the situation, but she was in no state to intervene. She had smoked a little and taken a hit of acid herself. Instead, she walked off toward her tent to chill for a while and await Mikko's return.

Sterling's laissez-faire attitude would be shattered about twenty minutes later when he and Flynn saw what they thought were sloping footprints up to the far rim of the canyon that disappeared over the other side. We decided Alyson should stay with Tilly to keep her calm while the rest of us hopped into Flynn's car and hauled ass down a dry creek bed toward where we though Mikko would have landed if he'd walked off the ledge. We searched for maybe fifteen minutes, but when we couldn't find Mikko's dead, broken body we figured things were alright for the time being.

So time passed. Alyson read by the fire pit as Flynn chilled nearby. Sterling decided to enjoy a beer in my hammock for the first time that trip. Tilly wandered up to the cliff where we thought Mikko may have fallen so as to keep a vigil for him. We yelled at her to stay on this side. She mumbled, "Alright," and somehow through the acoustics of the canyon it carried right to us.

I decided to take some time for myself. I climbed the wall of the canyon across from Tilly. We were both in our own little world and didn't pay much attention to each other. I found a nice outcrop to sit down and meditate on a few things. After twenty minutes or so I made my way down, leaping a few yards at a time. The last sixty feet was an all out run / jump / slide through a shale field that livened my spirits. I walked back to camp invigorated and ready for the evening. That feeling must have been what drew Mikko to sprint up and down the canyon walls the day before. I would find out later that during my entire descent Tilly had hallucinated I was still at the top of the canyon. My actual personage appeared to her as a coyote leaping down the rocks. It was an interesting topic of conversation as we recounted the events of the day.

Eventually Mikko made his way back to camp a bit disheveled and missing a sock. He explained to us that, in his altered state, he had decided he needed to find the perfect place to drop a deuce. The quest took him on a wandering search of the entire surrounding area for the better part of an hour. At last he did find such a perfect spot, only to realize he hadn't brought any toilet paper. Hence the missing sock. As is so often the case, the reality of the situation was much more bizarre than any of us had imagined.

Dinner was spaghetti with canned pasta sauce, which was delicious after a day of hard work. We had originally intended to open a bottle of wine, but somehow we couldn't find a corkscrew in the entire campsite. Thus, dinner was relatively dry. We tried to estimate how many Man Points we had accrued climbing Vader Rock. The final decision was somewhere in the range of ten thousand each.

Mikko and Tilly were still feeling some effects of the acid, so I decided it was as good a time as any to break out a few glow sticks I had brought. Tilly spent the next half hour completely entranced by the ebb and flow of the luminescent liquid. After a few minutes being lost to the world, she would suddenly demand a new color. Once she had another glow stick in hand, she would hurl her previous one with all her strength at whomsoever she felt was worthy of receiving it. Then again she would become consumed by the fluorescent device. At one point Flynn gathered all four sticks, bound them together with some twine, and handed them back to Tilly. She turned it over and over again as she marveled at the rainbow in her hands. It was a spectacle of unfiltered joy. Laugh as I might, it was something worth experiencing.

So the night passed without incident. I decided to stay up to watch the fire die out after everyone else had made for their sleeping bags. It was probably around 2:30 AM when I called it quits. We had burnt about half of our store of firewood and saved the other half for the next night with the intent to build a fire to the heavens.

The following morning we woke to thrashing winds. At first we thought it was just a minor annoyance, but sometime over breakfast we heard a tremendous snap come from Alyson's tent. We looked over to see the whole thing collapse in ruin. One of the poles had broken rendering it unusable. Together we helped Alyson tear it down lest it suffer more damage. Some of us worked on packing up the pieces while the others just held on so it wouldn't blow away in the wind.

Flynn bid us farewell and set off for Minnesota once that was done. He had missed enough class already and needed to get back to school. Sterling laid out two options for the rest of us. Such high winds usually blew in rain, which would make for a very sobering night. We could either soldier through the wind and possibly rain then break camp the next morning, or end the trip a day early and make for Colorado.

With the threat of rain on the horizon we were fine with losing the extra day. We made a quick strike and were on the road within the hour. Alyson would ride with Sterling as he made a beeline for home. Mikko and Tilly would accompany me to Moab where I had some business to attend to.

As we set off, Sterling stuck with me until we were past the four-wheeling section. Once he was sure I had made it through safe and sound he pulled his car up to mine for one final goodbye. In that moment I was struck with what Sterling had been able to accomplish. Years later, when I was taking my own family on a similar excursion, I found myself trying to emulate the sort of leadership he had demonstrated at only nineteen. When we were all very much still children, he had organized and led the lot of us into the desert, hours from civilization, with the confidence and ability to bring us out again. That was the day I finally saw Sterling for the man he was. A man who could always deliver on his word. A man who I had every confidence in.

I might have said all this to him if I had known it was the last time we would road trip together for more than a decade. Instead, I called through the window, "Where to now, fearless leader?"

He just laughed, as if I was joking.

2

The prior year I made a similar trip with Dean and Alan out to Canyonlands. It was a family vacation at heart. About nine kids and nearly as many adults all convened in Moab then made our way to a campsite in Canyonlands proper. That meant we were packed shoulder to shoulder with a hundred other folks out for some family fun over spring break. We spent our days hiking through the desert, and we spent our nights roasting hotdogs and s'mores over the fire. The parents all talked shop, rattling off the relative pros and cons of their new camp stoves, tents, what have you. They had all been camping together for years. As this was my first trip with the group I listened to all the cautionary tales of years past. On one outing a guy slipped a disc while riding in the back of a pickup across rutted out roads, then still had to suffer through the eight hour ride back to Colorado. Another year rangers found the kids disturbing crypto soil, the microbe-laden ground cover that's fundamental for all life in the region, and made them do community service as punishment.

The camping itself was a rather mundane affair. Dean had the reins of his own car though, so our time on the interstate felt like our own adventure. If there was one indelible truth about Dean it's that he was a hellion at the wheel. His dad once said he drove like a cowboy and damned if it wasn't true. He drove wearing a pair of ski goggles so he could shove his entire head out the open window and feel the full force of the wind on his face. He would offhandedly remark during our trip to Canyonlands, "Fuck, I'm going ninety again." Looking back, that's probably why I was so preoccupied with my own land speed record the following year.

On our way back to Colorado we spent a night in Glenwood Springs and decided to hit the hot springs. It was a cold night and steam billowed off the surface of the water clouding our vision. Being immature high school boys, we began musing about what would happen if a babe approached us through the mists. Just then a gust of wind blew purposefully over our heads, parting the cloud in front of us just so to reveal a bear of a man, both in stature and body hair, who had the word "BABE" tattooed in block letters across his back. I suppose we should have been more careful what we wished for.

That's not the real story from the trip though. Dean was a man whose freewheeling spirit could infect those around him. At least, that's how I like to preface this story as it makes it seem like I'm not to blame for my actions. We were about a half hour from the nearest town when Alan announced he needed to pee. He told us that we had to pull over because he couldn't wait. Dean said no. His counter offer: Alan should dangle himself out the window and relieve his bladder while we drove. I wholeheartedly agreed. After a good two minutes of goading, in which I thought it was about to happen, Alan finally laid down the law. There was no way that he was peeing out the window of a car driving at seventy-five mph. I was pretty disheartened to hear Alan's resolve. As far as I was concerned this was an experience that at least one of us needed to have in our lives. If Alan was not going to do it, then dammit I would. I won't detail all the logistics behind how I managed it, primarily because I don't want anyone to ever try imitating it. It was incredibly stupid and goes to show that it's a wonder I survived my teenage years. Suffice to say the deed was done and leave it at that.

So why am I even mentioning this? Is it one of those stories of triumph that I alluded to in the preface? I wouldn't exactly describe it as a triumph. No, I included this story to illustrate the aura that surrounded Dean and all that he did. Being with Dean meant being a part of outrageous experiences. Case in point, the following tale was a favorite during our high school days, and is another that should never be imitated by anyone. I wasn't present for this event, so I can't say for sure that it occurred as I am about to describe, nor that it even occurred at all. But then again, who's to say that any of the stories in this book actually took place? Either way, it's a tale worth telling. It came to me through Ray who happened to be one of the passengers in the car at the time.

Dean, like all of us young men who were enamored with the possibilities offered by a full tank of gas, was fond of driving around town with no real destination in mind. On one such drive, he and a few friends were prowling the westernmost streets of Boulder. That was the area where the city began climbing into the mountains. The streets that run parallel to the foothills are level so that drivers don't risk sliding across the road on icy days. The cross streets that intersect them are all sloped downward on account of the foothills smoothing out into the valley below. Being as they were already a ways into the foothills, the cross streets along their path were extremely inclined. Now that I have established the particular geography of the roadway, allow me to elaborate on the insanity that was to ensue.

As Ray told it, they happened upon one particularly inspiring intersection. That was where Dean allegedly stopped the car, sat for a few seconds, then instructed everyone to, "Buckle up boys." Sensing something momentous and life threatening was about to occur, everyone immediately complied. It's a good thing too, as more than likely Dean would have proceeded regardless. He then threw the car in reverse and backed his way more than two hundred yards up the heavily sloped cross street in order to build a sufficient runway. Once he reached the pinnacle of his ascent, he threw the car into drive and began speeding toward the intersection.

What happened next was a scene that I've pictured a thousand times in my mind. What, I wonder, must it have felt like when the road abruptly transitioned from a seven-percent grade to dead level? Would I be aware of the sensation of my spine suddenly compressing as the ground lurched up into the vehicle? What would the shock absorbers sound like as they compressed to their physical limit? Was it an awful crunch as metal was thrust against metal? Or an ear piercing rasp as the aged mechanisms twisted against each other to combat the impact? Or perhaps it was simply a sickening thud as the entire front end collapsed further than it was ever meant to?

I'm afraid I can't say for sure. I wasn't there to see if the frontend sent a spray of sparks as it scraped through the intersection. I don't know how much force the shocks exerted back into the car as it bottomed out. I didn't experience the nauseating feeling in the pit of my stomach as the street fell away from the tires. I can only imagine all of this as Dean adamantly refused to ever repeat the endeavor. To hear Ray tell the story though, to hear him describe the moment the earth rushed up to meet him and subsequently thrust the entire vehicle into the sky, I could almost imagine I was right there with him.

As I said before, I don't know if this truly did happen. But do I believe with every fiber of my being that it did? Yes. Yes I do. I do for a number of reasons, not the least of which being that Dean had little compunction when it came to leaving portions of his car on the road. On a separate evening the two of us had been hiking in the foothills. We left Dean's car at a parking lot rimmed with boulders that must have weighed a few hundred pounds each. As we were pulling out Dean was a little overconfident in his car's turning radius and tagged one of the boulders on the passenger side. By that I mean that he smashed the bumper of his car so hard I was lifted about four inches off the ground. We stopped to inspect the damage and found that the front skid plate had come loose on one side but seemed to be holding. Since we didn't have any tools to repair the front end we decided to drive on. Everything was fine for the first few miles, but something happened when we hit the ramp from Baseline to US-36. I'm not sure if it had to do with the sudden acceleration or some especially large bump, but the next thing we heard was a terrible sound of plastic being rent apart. I stuck my head out the window to see what had happened. There in the middle of the ramp was the roughly six-foot long plastic skid plate. It must have gotten sucked under the front tire and torn away by the momentum of the car. We drove on and made no mention of it to anyone.

Beyond all history of vehicular mayhem though, what led me to believe every word of Ray's story was the awe-inspiring nature of Dean's presence. To experience Dean was to experience things I never thought possible. There were not many people that had as deep and profound of an effect on my development as Dean did. Sometimes it was through his own actions and other times it was through those that he attracted to his orbit.

Years later I found myself spending a week wandering the streets of New York City with him as I prepared to fulfill one of my adolescent dreams. After years of being officially broken up, Rage Against The Machine was scheduled to headline the Rock The Bells festival at Randall's Island. When Dean heard this he knew he had to be there, and he easily convinced Mikko, Tilly, and myself to join him. We scraped together the money we had from a year of adulthood, bought our plane tickets, and flew out east. We booked a tiny room in a hostel just a few blocks from Central Park for the first few days. It had a single bunk bed and we had to turn sideways to walk between it and the opposing wall. Tilly and Mikko were going to stay at his aunt's house in Brooklyn, but we pulled into town too late for that, so the very first night we had Mikko and Tilly in the top bunk with Dean and I in the bottom.

The following days were spent lounging about Manhattan. We hit up the Whitney Museum for a psychedelic seventies exhibit, wandered through Central Park, whatever we felt like really. Each morning Dean and I would grab a quick breakfast somewhere, figure out a spot to meet up with Tilly and Mikko, spend eight hours doing our thing, then Tilly and Mikko would head back on the train and Dean and I would find something to entertain us for the evening. It was a pleasant routine.

On one such evening Dean and I found ourselves wandering through Little Italy with a cavity in our bellies that we wished to fill. By happenstance we stopped in front of a restaurant that was thumping. I couldn't say what made us think to stop there, but to our surprise we were not turned away outright when we inquired with the maître d'. He muttered something about being completely full, but then he cast a glance to a man behind us that we had failed to notice when we walked up. Both Dean and I turned to find a slender gentleman with mostly gray hair that was quite becoming in his entirely white suit. The gold chain around his neck and the sunglasses he so brazenly wore in the dead of night told us he was a man of respect around the area.

He caught the eye of the maître d' then confidently strode forward and placed one hand on Dean's back and the other on mine. Without a word he ushered us into the restaurant. A quick motion from him sent a bus boy scurrying to set up a heretofore unseen table and chairs. After the man of respect had seated us he strolled out of the restaurant. Dean and I had no idea what had transpired just then but we knew one thing for sure: at that point we wouldn't be allowed to eat anywhere else even if we wanted to.

That was just one instance of the odd effects Dean seemed to conjure whenever I was around him. I could never be sure exactly what was going to happen, but something always did, and I was always glad to be a part of it. I guess I would call them character building experiences. Moments that I never expected but that served to enrich my life. Another night during that same trip, the four of us were walking down an unassuming street in Manhattan. To this day I have no idea how the following interaction was initiated. What I first noticed was Tilly walking up to an ordinary woman standing outside a jewelry shop, motioning to the hand bag she held, and asking the woman something that sounded like, "Do you have any of these?"

The next thing I knew, this very normal woman hurried into the jewelry store with the clear expectation that we would follow close behind. She led us straight to the far wall of the shop and quickly knocked a brief cadence on it. Immediately a crack appeared in the very ordinary wall, then it widened into a large doorway leading into a tiny room filled with other women. At this point I began to back away, thinking I could avoid participating in whatever was about to happen and instead pretend to inspect the normal wares of the shop. The woman who led us there was having none of that and pulled me into the tiny back room after Dean, Mikko, and Tilly. As soon as I was inside the door slammed shut behind me, once again forming a seamless plane with the wall around it.

As my eyes adjusted to the dim lighting I realized that the room only felt small because it was crammed with very convincing counterfeit purses. Two women stood inside, one to work the door and the other to locate products throughout the makeshift warehouse. While I was still taking in our surroundings Tilly was presenting her purse to the latter of the two women. After a quick examination she began digging through the mountain of knockoffs. Less than a minute later she produced a bag that I would have sworn up and down was an actual Gucci. Tilly paid the woman a small roll of cash and, after a brief peek outside to ensure the coast was clear, we were ushered back to the street. We were perhaps two or three blocks away before any of us asked how in the world Tilly had keyed in on that operation. She shrugged off the question without giving us any real answer. I suppose some people just have the knack for that sort of thing, and Dean tended to draw those people to himself.

Dean was the core of a very eclectic group of folks that I called my friends. I spent nearly every day for three years sitting around his basement or free-wheeling with him about town. Dean created an environment in which all of us were free to be our true selves. That swirl of individuality always led to bizarre and wonderful moments.

I sometimes have trouble explaining who Dean was and what he meant to me growing up. I recently tried to detail his philosophies to a friend only to have her exclaim that Dean sounded like a cult leader. Maybe that's not far from the truth, or maybe I don't do him justice. In case it's the latter, I'll let him speak for himself. This is an excerpt from a letter he wrote to Ray and I as we set off for college, just a few months after that urine fueled trip to Utah:

> Now I could write you guys sappy going away letters, but in your guys' case I think, or at least I hope that you know damn well that I love the both of you, and I'm going to be 30 minutes away, so there really isn't much of a going away. So what I have decided to do

instead is write up a list of requests if you want to establish your dorm room as a franchise of this basement. [...] Everyone in the dorm should legitimately care about each other, that's what makes a group a group. There should be a wide variety of types of people often housed in your dorm. [...] The dorm should be universally welcoming to anyone on campus who comes with the intent simply to become friends. [...] Finally and most importantly the friendships you establish at college better be just as high quality as the bond shared by the tremendous six over the past 2 or 3 years. [...] Remember that whatever circles we find ourselves rolling with in college we are still one another's roots.

The letter was both a goodbye and a toast to adventures yet to come. I keep it on the bookshelf in my office to remember the ethos that brought so many of us together. Authenticity, honesty, and a drive to always find the best in people. Those were the qualities that invariably drew me to Dean.

3

March of 2012 would see me in the wilds of Utah one more time. True to style, this trip would include no one from either of my previous ventures. I had hoped to make it out with Sterling to recreate the journey from our freshman year of college, but we couldn't work out the logistics. Instead, Sterling suggested I call up Lucas as he was planning a trip somewhere near Vader Rock. I got ahold of him, but found out he didn't have room in his car, nor even any time for us to get together and talk through the trip in person. Instead he sent me an email with the dates he would be camping, a satellite image of some BLM land with an X to roughly mark the campsite, and an earnest wish that he would see me out there before the trip was done.

At that point I had everything I needed except a car. By my approximation The Icebox wasn't going to make another journey, so I needed another vehicle that could withstand the trek through a few miles of rutted dirt roads. Sterling was out as I already mentioned, and most other folks had much more pedestrian vehicles. As luck would have it though, Liam was coming to town around that time and would have access to his parents CR-V. He had graduated from the Air Force ROTC program two years prior and had been stationed in Texas doing mundane work for the government ever since. He was taking leave and wanted to see as many people as possible, so we decided that he would make a quick stint to see his family and a large contingent of friends then we would hit the road west. Since he only had a few days he could be off base we had to make it quick. We would set out on a Monday morning and be back that Wednesday night.

The best route I could find to get us to the campsite almost exactly traced the journey I had taken with Sterling five years prior. We would head west on I-70 past Green River then jog south for a ways, but we would eventually backtrack east toward Canyonlands to find our campsite. That's where things got a little hairy as the dirt roads we needed didn't appear on any maps we could find online. Fortunately I still had a GPS signal on my phone and the forethought to pull up the satellite view in my maps app, which traced a little blue dot along the path we traveled. I compared our progress to the screenshot Lucas had sent me the week before and charted a course to the camp while Liam picked his way in between herds of grazing cattle. The last few miles were through the most rutted dirt roads I'd ever seen. The grass growing in the center of the road persistently scrubbed the undercarriage. More than once we had to stop the car to clear rocks out of our path. Eventually we made it through and were received by Lucas and maybe a half dozen of his friends who had arrived at the site a day or two prior. We had just enough light to pitch our tent and then we settled in for a night of drunken revelry by the campfire.

Utah camping could never be complete without whiskey and beer, but that would only keep us so warm. Lucas had already stoked a mighty fire and we kept it roaring the whole night long. Around 11:00 PM we took stock of each other, asking if it was time for bed or if we should add another commitment log. Of course we were all eager to keep going, so we threw another five-inch-thick log on the fire. It fell to ash over the course of a few hours as we dwindled in numbers. I took the long shift with Liam and one other guy watching the last logs burn out. We turned in around 2:00 AM.

Tuesday was our day to explore. Lucas knew some trails in the area, so half the crew piled into his Highlander and the rest of us clambered into Liam's CR-V. We backtracked to the main dirt road as there was only one way in or out of the campsite, and headed past a nearby ranger station. We soon arrived at a trailhead somewhere in Canyonlands. The hike was pleasant with a number of beautiful views. It dipped a bit through a very open air canyon where we found a nice spot to eat lunch and discussed our plans for the rest of the day. We were less than halfway through one giant loop and ultimately decided to head back to the campsite for more debauchery.

We had a good evening in store for us, though I fell into my classic stick in the mud mode. Liam and I had drunk more than our share during our late watch the night before, and Liam was up for doing it all over again. I was more concerned that our stores of water were running low and I didn't want to be dehydrated and hungover in the morning trying to break camp and make the drive back to Colorado. In the end I crawled into the tent early to get some sleep while the rest of the party raged outside. We only had two nights in the desert and I had squandered one.

In the morning we breakfasted and hit the road. We convoyed out of the campsite and snapped one last group photo by the park sign. From there we made good time across Utah and into western Colorado. Nearly too good as we crested an incline just east of the border only to see a state trooper looking for speeders at the base of the hill. Our entire party, along with another three or four nearby cars, all slammed our brakes at once to drop from a hot ninety to a respectable seventy-seven mph. For whatever reason, the trooper didn't see fit to pull anyone over.

It reminded me of a time years earlier when a trooper had us dead to rights but chose not to ticket us. Liam was at the wheel as a group of us were traveling west on I-70 for a much anticipated ski trip. As we exited the Eisenhower tunnel we were met with a stout blowing snow. Visibility wasn't great, but it wasn't that bad yet either. The storm must have just been starting as the roads weren't any more slick than usual. There were only a few cars on the road, so Liam was going at a decent clip down the mountain. It was a little over the limit and arguably too fast for the conditions. That's certainly how the patrolman felt.

At first we didn't think much of the highway patrol car that pulled up beside us and maintained our exact pace. We figured that if we had done anything wrong he would have flashed his lights and pulled us over. That was until we heard what sounded like a man's voice speaking outside. Perplexed, we rolled down our windows to discover the cop had gotten on his loud speaker and begun shouting harassments at us. It was difficult to understand everything he was saying as we flew down the highway with our windows open, but we all picked out the phrase, "Are you unintelligent? Slow down!" Needless to say we did.

Back to the story at hand. We found a Mongolian BBQ place in Grand Junction and decided that was just what everyone needed to drive away the last remnants of our hangovers. We watched piles of meat roast on swords in front of our eyes then took it to go so we could eat on a little berm outside. It was the most grass we'd seen in days. We chatted awhile then parted ways. Lucas was eager to make it home as quick as possible whereas Liam and I were moving more leisurely.

We had one last spot of trouble making our way east through Colorado. As we approached the Eisenhower tunnel, actually the Johnson tunnel but no one differentiates the two, the engine started screeching. We calmly pulled off where HazMat trucks queue up just outside the tunnel and got to work diagnosing the problem. We didn't make much fuss about the situation, probably because this wasn't the first time the two of us had broken down on the side of the highway.

In the spring of 2006 Liam and I were driving from Denver to Boulder along I-25 when the road became inexplicably bumpy. We both made offhand comments about how terrible the conditions were without any thought of investigating the matter further. That was until I started to see little chunks of black material flying away from the side of the car. I rolled down the window to get a better look and discovered that one of the tires was completely flat.

Liam pulled over in the first available area, which happened to be the right side of the exit ramp from I-25 to US-36. I had about twenty inches between my door and the retaining wall. That was space enough to climb out without much trouble. Liam only had about five inches between his door and interstate traffic, so he had to pick his exit a little more carefully. As such, I was the first to discover the sidewall of his rear, passenger-side tire had completely blown out. There was a gash about five inches long exposing the metal mesh inlaid in the rubber, which made the process of changing the wheel that much more difficult. We would each cut ourselves on that mesh before the deed was done.

Liam had a spare in the trunk of his car, though it was buried under two sets of golf clubs because that's the sort of man Liam was. Just after we got everything unloaded I received a call from Ray to see if we were okay. He and a few other friends had been hanging with us in Denver and they were just passing us on their way home. Our conversation went something like this:

"Hello?"
"Dude, are you and Liam pulled over on the side of the road?"
"Yep."
"What happened?"
"Liam blew a tire."
"...That sucks."
"Yep.
"Well, is there anything we can do?"
"No, I think we've got this."
"Ok, see you back in Boulder."
"See ya."

By then Liam had the car on the jack and was starting to unscrew the lug nuts. We pulled off the flat and lined up the spare tire. That was when we discovered we had only raised the car enough to remove the flat. We would need another couple minutes to crank it even higher and finish the job. All the while our car was shaking every time another car drove by, threatening to come crashing down on the bare metal. I nearly crapped myself the first time a semi came rushing by with its massive air wash.

We managed to swap the tire and get everything stowed again without incident. That still left us with the small matter of merging back into traffic. As I said we were on the right hand side of the ramp between I-25 and US-36. In reality US-36 begins as I-25 and I-270 converge, and we were smack dab between the two with only about a hundred feet before the shoulder disappeared entirely. Liam had to keep his head on a swivel to ensure we didn't get side-swiped from either side as he punched it to sixty-five as hard as he could. He found a gap in traffic, and the spare didn't fall off the axel in the process, so we were home free.

Our breakdown on I-70 required a less straightforward fix though. We scanned the engine and noticed one of the belts had gone slack. We traced its path and discovered a tensioner had snapped its bearing and was wedged deep in the engine block. The belt was still tight enough that it was spinning the broken tensioner causing the screeching sound as it scraped against the rest of the machinery.

After some contortion work to keep from burning our hands we managed to yank out the broken tensioner. From there we had to determine if the car was still roadworthy. We looked up the engine diagram in the manual and traced the belt system. Luckily we had only lost one of the ancillary belts that powered the AC compressor. No big deal, it just meant a hot drive down to Boulder. We pulled the belt itself out as well so it wouldn't hook on any other moving part and finished the trip without further incident.

I'll admit that driving out to Utah for only two nights was a pretty ridiculous endeavor just to have some time with Liam and the gang. That said, I've done a lot more for the chance to see Liam. In the fall of 2006 we had all begun our freshman year of college. Liam had gone to Kansas State in search of a good architecture program and a strong ROTC culture. What he discovered when he got there was that he hated everything about Kansas. When he had an extended weekend a month and a half into the semester he was desperate to come back for a visit. Trouble was he didn't have a car nor any other real means to make the trip. That was when a bunch of us hatched a plan to get him home.

Once Liam was done with classes on Friday he would board a westbound Greyhound bus. Meanwhile, Ray and Sterling would head east out of Boulder by car. The three of them would rendezvous in Colby, Kansas then immediately head toward Boulder. I desperately wanted to be a part of the trip, but I couldn't get off work that night. Thus it happened that I was hanging out in Dean's basement at 11:24 PM when Liam burst down the stairs and tackled Dean in his excitement to be back in Colorado.

That enthusiasm carried us late into the night. We spent a long while sitting around catching up. Ray and Sterling both remarked how wild it was that just a few hours earlier they were in Kansas, and a few hours before that they had been in Colorado. Eventually we set out for a night hike through the foothills. An admittedly stupid thing to do as just about everyone I've known has seen a mountain lion out there at one time or another, but we were young and invincible. Sometime around two or three in the morning we crashed Lucas's place to sit in the hot tub for a bit, then it was time to call it a night.

Liam didn't feel like going home, and Sterling's roommate had made it clear that there was a girl in the room that night and he should make other sleeping arrangements. Thus it was decided that the four of us would crash in the 120-square-foot dorm room that Ray and I shared. I've previously mentioned that many of the dorm rooms had broken or faulty appliances. In our case, the phone had never worked. There was no dial tone when we picked up the receiver even though, as we would soon learn, the phone line itself was perfectly intact. So as we were all settling in for the night Liam decided to dial 9-1-1 then hang up because, and I quote, he had, "Never dialed 9-1-1 before." He just wanted to give it a shot.

Ray and I were annoyed but we didn't press the matter too much as the phone was ostensibly broken. Shortly thereafter we all fell asleep, which meant we were all in roughly the same exhausted stupor when someone began banging on the door forty-five minutes later. No one was exactly fast to answer until we heard the person on the other side shout, "Open up, police." Sterling jumped up and let the officer in. She did a quick scan of the room to make sure everyone was alright then left with a warning. Ray seemed furious, but Liam just laughed the whole thing off. All I could say was, thank God there wasn't an actual emergency. A forty-five minute response time did not exactly inspire confidence.

The rest of the weekend was spent in much the same way as the first night, sans any more fake calls to 9-1-1. We spent most of our time exploring the mountains that Liam so sorely missed while in Kansas. Eventually Monday rolled around and Liam needed to head back to school. Those of us at CU did not have the day off, so Sterling and I went to our respective classes then met up with Liam around 3:00 PM. Unlike the trip from Kansas to Colorado, Liam wouldn't be able to split his time driving with us and taking a Greyhound. Sterling and I would have to make a fifteen hour marathon drive all the way to Kansas State and back in one night.

Sterling's folks were kind enough to loan us their Acura for the trip as none of us had a vehicle that could get there and back without requiring outrageous amounts of gas. We hit the tollway out of town then caught I-70 heading east. No one was all that excited to be on the road toward Manhattan, Kansas, so we entertained ourselves as best we could. Liam found a multitude of umbrellas and began stroking us with them from the backseat much to our chagrin. Somewhere near Strasburg, Colorado, the three of us marveled at a man with a mullet riding a motorcycle while also snacking on a box of cherry tomatoes of all things.

Our initial tank of gas took us as far as Limon, Colorado, where we decided to pull off and stretch our legs. The Shell station we stopped at connected to a decent sized minimart and offered us the potential for some distractions. I pumped a couple quarters into a claw machine and came away with nothing to show for it. Sterling resisted the urge to buy a three pound bag of gummy bears that was prominently advertised in the window. After we had thoroughly explored the building we sat down for dinner and watched a rather pleasant sunset.

Neither Sterling nor I considered the possibility that we could still be in Kansas the next time we saw the sun, though that would prove to be the reality of our trip.

After dinner we got back on I-70. Liam was driving with Sterling riding shotgun while I was in the backseat. Sterling had just downloaded a real-time navigation app on his phone and he proceeded to look up directions to Manhattan. Keep in mind that this was nearly a year before the first iPhone was released, so none of us had ever received live directions from a phone before. Thus, when it announced in a matter-of-fact tone that we were to stay on I-70 for another 370 miles we all burst out laughing. In that moment it finally dawned on us what we had gotten ourselves into.

With a few hundred miles of road ahead of us we found more juvenile ways to pass the time. Liam had bought a toy from one of those gumball style machines at the gas station. It was a little eyeball that would squish if we pressed on it then reinflate with a sickening sound. We amused ourselves by throwing it at the various car windows and watching it stick then slowly peel off, ready to be thrown again. That lasted until we challenged Sterling to stick it to the side of a semi as we passed. After his attempt we were left with just the plastic ball the eye had come in. Sterling filled that up with Pepsi and threw it as hard as he could in front of our own car. At first it seemed to be on a trajectory to hit the road ahead of us. A moment later it appeared suspended in air, as we steadily caught up to it. Then it propelled toward us at an alarming speed and detonated on our windshield, much to our delight.

As we neared the Kansas border we discovered something very odd about Colorado. I-70 stretched 436 miles across the state. However, there was no mile marker 420. I wasn't sure if the lawmakers rejected that number altogether or if it was too enticing a target for people to steal. I had trouble believing the latter as their alternative seemed like much more of a target. Instead of marking mile 420, the powers that be placed a 419.99 marker one one-hundredth of a mile to the west.

Sterling decided he wanted to take a nap shortly after we crossed the state line, but we had been sternly cautioned by his parents that the person riding shotgun should never nap during a drive as that could lull the driver to sleep. Believing that to be true, we decided it would be best if Sterling and I switched places. The intelligent course of action would have been to pull off and quickly make the change, but we were still in the mood for juvenile entertainment. We instead decided to make the switch while Liam kept pace along the interstate. I moved out of the way the best I could as Sterling climbed over the center console, then I advanced forward in the same way trying my best not to kick Sterling in the face or cause Liam to crash the car. Liam and I feigned conversation for fifteen minutes or so before Sterling popped back up and declared he wasn't going to get any sleep anyway.

That was shortly before we arrived at WaKeeney, Kansas, where we stopped to fill up the tank and clean the Pepsi off the hood. From there it was my turn to take the wheel. We had been goading each other throughout the drive to see who could go the fastest during their shift. I averaged about ninety with my top speed peaking at just over a hundred. Sterling was a bit higher. Liam was a bit lower. Somehow none of us got ticketed in spite of the seventy mile per hour speed limit in Kansas. I suppose I should say none of us got ticketed on the trip east.

The rest of the drive was long but uneventful. Some philosophical conversation took place for a moment but we were mostly shooting the shit. We pulled into Manhattan well after midnight and headed straight for KSU campus. Liam took us around to a few lecture halls and then to his design studio. He showed us various sketches and a model he was making of a church. He explained all the tools of the trade to us. I listened intently while Sterling scrawled something to the effect of, "Liam is a sex god," on his work desk.

We discussed various subjects related to architecture for a while longer then decided to retire to the Smith Scholarship House where Liam was living. The entrance was unassuming and littered with couches for the residents to lounge about. The sleeping quarters where Liam shared a room with three other guys were upstairs. Some intrepid students had built a loft over a portion of the room to maximize the space. It was a rudimentary thing made of unfinished two-by-fours and particleboard. It's important to note that the ceiling was only about eight feet high in the room, so there was hardly any space below or above the loft. The loft itself was reserved as a sort of lounge area. It contained an eclectic collection of arm chairs, each with its feet removed to accommodate the low ceiling. The area underneath was designated as a study room in which Liam would jostle with the three other tenants assigned to the quarters, each trying to garner enough desk space to do his homework.

Liam made a special point of showing us the bizarre design of the shared bathroom that adjoined the living quarters. The room itself was roughly split in half by a partial wall. The area nearest the door had the toilets against the full wall and sinks on the partial wall. The far side of the room had all the showers, which were hardly obscured by the partial wall, leaving them in full view of anyone walking by while the door was opened. That wouldn't have been such a big deal except that there were absolutely no privacy barriers in the entire bathroom. The showers didn't have curtains and the toilets didn't have stalls. That little detail also meant that Liam could, and frequently would, make inadvertent eye contact with his dormmates in the mirror as he washed his hands and they did their business. Any thoughts Sterling and I had of relieving ourselves before the drive home quickly dissipated.

Our tour then wound to one of the shared workrooms in the house, where we found two of Liam's dormmates toiling away. Although they had a long weekend to finish their Calculus homework they had naturally procrastinated until after midnight on the day it was due. We chatted with them awhile and they mentioned that the day before our arrival another resident had left for a drive and disappeared for hours. When he returned he declared he had driven all the way to the Colorado border for no particular reason. A man after my own heart.

We left them to their work and headed down to the rec room in the basement. I fancied myself a strong pool player in those days, so I challenged Sterling to a dollar-a-ball game when we discovered a table down there. He refused outright. We instead spent our time examining photos on the wall of previous graduating classes, marveling at their ridiculous styles. Next we toured the kitchen where we saw Liam had been assigned the task of baking cookies every Friday. Next was the laundry room where Liam remarked he had always wondered what was behind a certain door that remained padlocked at all times. As luck would have it, I had a set of lock picks in my backpack and I took Liam's remark as a challenge. He was reluctant to permit such impropriety at first, but he eventually allowed it after a little pestering. I worked the lock for a couple minutes and managed to make it through. Unfortunately behind that was another door with a warded lock, which I wasn't set up to handle. Some mysteries were not meant to be solved.

At 2:30 AM it was time for Sterling and I to set off. It would be a long journey back and we had class the next day. Liam had an ROTC fitness test in four hours so he needed some sleep as well. First though, we felt the need for one more bit of juvenile revelry. We circled up on the front lawn of Smith House for a traditional crotch thrust. Given how late it was we decided to be as quiet as possible, so we sounded off three barely audible grunts followed by a whispered, "Yeah!" We all nearly fell to the ground laughing at the absurdity of it. With the formalities properly observed we shared a heartfelt hug with Liam and hit the road.

I somehow convinced Sterling to look for a tattoo parlor in a misguided attempt to pick up a souvenir. Of course there was nothing open at that hour so we found our way back to the interstate and began retracing our steps west. Sterling took the first shift and I started off riding shotgun. We made small talk and listened to comedy on his iPod. Eventually the events of the night caught up with me, so I climbed into the backseat to nap until it was my turn at the wheel. I must have fallen asleep fast because it was just a few minutes before Sterling was waking me up as he was being pulled over.

The cop didn't seem phased that I had popped up in the middle of the backseat as Sterling swung us to the shoulder.

He had clocked us at seventy-seven in a sixty as we passed through a work zone, and he explained in no uncertain terms that he should double the fine even though the job site was completely abandoned at that hour. Instead he wrote a ticket for a little over a hundred dollars as Sterling had accelerated to eighty-seven in a seventy after he exited the work zone. From there we decided to tread lightly.

I slept for a while longer then crawled back into the front seat just as we reached our familiar gas station in WaKeeney. We filled up, traded places, and hit the road again. Earlier in the evening I was making grand plans to see if I could max out the speedometer, which would have been somewhere around a hundred and forty mph. Given what had happened to Sterling I made sure to keep my speed in the double-digit range. The sun started to rise in my rear view mirror as we neared the Colorado border, so we decided that was a good enough time to trade places again. We were keeping the shifts short to try to stay as rested as possible.

I slept for another few hours then woke up as we were pulling into a gas station in some tiny town. Since the sun was up attendants were starting to come to work, so Sterling decided it was time to restock the snacks. I waited in the car as he bought some jerky and energy drinks. The woman behind the register made some comment dripping with innuendo about chewing salty meat all night long. Maybe she was hitting on him, or maybe she was starting a long shift just hours after dawn broke and took the chance to mess with a delirious teenager. I'd believe either.

In our road-weary, bewildered state we somehow left the gas station without actually getting any gas. I had taken the wheel and didn't notice anything was amiss until the low gas light flicked on just minutes after I pulled onto the tollway to bypass Denver. That meant I had to get to an exit and then backtrack toward the city. We made it to the outskirts of town in a heavily industrial neighborhood with no gas stations in sight. I chose a direction and drove about six blocks before deciding things were getting more desolate that way. I pulled a u-turn and headed back the way I came for a couple miles. The needle was bouncing on E and still there was no place to fill up. I finally decided to pick a street that seemed to point toward the city center and drive until we found something or the tank ran dry. We lucked out and came across one as we were coasting on fumes. We filled up and decided our next move.

The night before Sterling and I had discussed dropping in on Dean's dorm unannounced on our way back. The morning was getting away from us though, so we decided to head straight for Boulder. Sterling was driving again while I got some sleep in the front seat. I had slept decently in the back, but I figured any risk of lulling Sterling to sleep had faded with the rising sun. Not to mention the seat warmer was calling my name. I woke up as we were merging onto US-36. We were well past rush hour, but pockets of bad traffic still lingered along the turnpike.

We arrived at campus just before 10:30 AM. Sterling dropped me at my dorm then drove off, presumably to return the car to his parents. I found Ray asleep in his bed where he had been soundly dreaming for a good nine hours. I dropped onto my bed for a couple hours of sleep before showering and heading off to my first class of the day.

That was the one and only time we made such a herculean journey to return Liam to Kansas, as he got a car of his own later that year. He ended up with a derelict Volvo 240 that had a quarter million miles on it when the odometer stopped working. Who knows how much road it had actually seen. The heater broke shortly after he bought it, so in the winter he would wear gloves, a hat, and a coat and still shiver the whole way between Boulder and Manhattan. He spent his first such trip trying to figure out what one of the gauges on his dash indicated, only to realize it was an analog clock. The car was a relic from a bygone era.

Liam made a strong effort to enjoy his time in Kansas, but after three semesters he had enough and transferred to the University of Colorado. He actually moved in with me when he came back to Boulder. That arrangement lasted exactly one semester as we butted heads a number of times. Liam had a cavalier attitude that could grate my nerves if I wasn't in the mood for his shenanigans. Even so, he was a steadfast friend that would gladly travel hundreds of miles if only for a weekend with the people he cared about, and I was happy to repay him in kind whenever I could. He graduated as a lieutenant in the Air Force and spent the next few years traveling the globe as a civil engineer for the military. Strangely, whether he was in Korea, Qatar, or the UK, he never seemed all that far away. I think that's because I knew I could count on him, no matter where he was in the world.

4

In the summer of 2015 Ray, Crystal, and I found ourselves with some extra free time during the Fourth of July weekend, so we decided to venture through all the portions of Colorado that we'd never seen before. We would head south toward the Great Sand Dunes then cut west toward Mesa Verde. From there we'd figure out a course home. The Fourth was on a Saturday that year, so we had the preceding Thursday and Friday off. As such, we hit the road on Wednesday night. We had a few good hours of daylight since it was so close to the solstice, but even so the sun had set by the time we hit Buena Vista. That was where we pulled off at a little gas station to restock our food and fuel.

I went inside to look for snacks while my companions were on fill up duty. Beef jerky was always a good staple since it could substitute for breakfast in a pinch. Some chips for carbs could be a lifesaver as well. I was weighing the options when Crystal and Ray came through the door and made a beeline for the clerk. Apparently the automatic shutoff valve for the pump didn't work, and gas had spilled all over the ground before they shut it off manually. The clerk decided to be a dick about it and blamed Crystal for not forcing the nozzle as deep in the tank as possible during the entire fill up process. Apparently it would have worked fine if she did that. I resisted the urge to make a snide comment about how he seemed to misunderstand the definition of working fine. The way I figured it, this was not the first nor the last time that night he would have to clean up gas because of that nozzle, and the thought of him rushing out to the pump every five minutes for an entire eight hour shift was retribution enough. All we had to do was pay and we were free to move on.

We made Alamosa in another hour or two and checked the weather report while we settled in to our room. I had stowed an old snowboard in the trunk so that I could finally try out a lifelong dream: I wanted to ride the dunes themselves. We had done some research before setting off and learned that traditional snowboards didn't often stand up well in the sand. There were specially designed sandboards and sand sleds with a wider base and different material to improve their ability to slide across sand. Snowboards tended to sink in and get trapped by friction. However, if there had been rain the day before to pack everything down then snowboards had a better chance at success. There hadn't been much precipitation that week, and none in the forecast for the next day, so chances were slim. Still I was undeterred.

The next morning we grabbed a hot breakfast from the hotel dining room. A shift toward providing hot meals seemed to be taking place at that time in the hospitality industry, and I was thoroughly a fan of it. Eggs and sausage while traveling did a great deal to lift my spirits. A biscuit and gravy were even better. They were never high quality, but they stuck to the ribs and when I didn't hunger for food I hungered for the road all the more.

After filling our bellies we headed straight for the sand dunes themselves. When there's been enough moisture over the summer a small rivulet forms between the northern border of the dunes and the parking lots. It was in full swing when we arrived, and local families had arrived to play in the cool waters and leave the rest of the national park to the tourists. Crystal waded the creek without issue as she was the only one with the foresight to bring boots on the expedition. Ray and I kicked off our shoes and we set off toward the nearest dune. As we approached we could see a few folks with sand sleds burning down the slope. I almost regretted my decision not to do the same, but I had to know if a snowboard would actually work. At a distance the dunes looked pretty hard packed, which gave me hope for the trial to come.

I soon discovered it was nearly impossible to charge straight up a dune unhindered, let alone trying to carry a snowboard on my back. I had to zigzag my way up, creating my own switchbacks when I veered too far off course. Ray and Crystal trudged up in a similar manner. Once the three of us reached the top I hardly paused to take in the view before dropping to strap on my board. I had salvaged an old pair of bindings specifically for this purpose. They had fit my snowboard boots when I was about nine years old. As an adult they were only a bit too large on my feet when I was wearing regular shoes. Turning and stopping would not be easy with my feet free to wiggle that much, but that was no problem. On my first ride my speed held steady at a comfortable clip even when tracing a straight line down the dune. It was a little pedestrian compared to a ski resort but fun overall.

I got to the bottom, undid the bindings, and once again crisscrossed my way back up to the party. Ray proposed that we head deeper into the park to where we could feel like we were the only ones around. Turns out we didn't have to venture very far. All the fair-weather tourists made it to the summit of the nearest dune and felt accomplished. If we just went one or two back we were in a world by ourselves.

The rest of the morning was rather pleasant. We snapped some photos of the majesty all around us. I did a few more runs, and Ray and Crystal gave it a go as well. After a couple hours we began to discover the areas on our bodies that we had missed with sunscreen. I had a spot on the back of either arm just below my sleeves that had turned bright red and started to itch. With that we decided it was time to get out of the sun. We hiked back to the car and hit the road toward Durango. The plan was to spend the night there and then check out Mesa Verde the following morning.

We grabbed some lunch and headed west along US-160. At this point we'd entered uncharted territory for me. I had never been in the quadrant west of Alamosa and south of I-70 in the state in my life. I drank in the landscape. More than once we found ourselves compelled to pull off at a scenic overlook and take in the view. As we drove we discussed the prospect of meeting up with Laura while we were in Durango. None of us had talked to her in years. In fact, Crystal may not have ever met her before. Still, Ray and I spent most of our high school days hanging out with her, and that bond ran deep. I didn't have her number so I looked her up on Facebook and explained the situation. Turned out she was more than excited to meet up. I estimated when we would get to town and set up a dinner at one of the breweries in Durango.

We eventually made it to town, dropped our bags at the hotel, and set off to meet our childhood friend. She had her hubby and new baby in tow, but the babe slept through the entirety of dinner even with the clatter of a hopping brewery on a Thursday night rising all around her. I wondered if I would be so lucky when I finally started having kids. We had a lively dinner with or without a conscious baby to fawn over. None of us had met Laura's husband before, so we learned all about him and his work. He was on the path of taking over the family business and had begun expanding it to different realms. They'd just opened a distillery a year or two before and there were plenty of exasperated stories to go along with that adventure.

We continued our conversation for an hour or two before it was time to put the baby to bed. We said our goodbyes then decided to explore the town a bit on our own. Businesses were closing up by that hour, but we found an ice cream shop that was profiting off the late night sugar cravers and decided to treat ourselves. We turned in shortly after that as we were finally feeling our travels.

The next day we woke and continued westward. We made Mesa Verde in about an hour and booked a tour of the Cliff Palace for later that morning. We spent some time wandering the area learning about the society that built the dwelling ages ago. I tried to avoid the sun as much as possible as the burns on my arms had been throbbing all morning. Eventually the tour started and we spent about an hour walking through the cliff dwellings themselves. There were large ceremonial pits called kivas dug about eight feet deep into the floor of one dwelling. Despite warnings from the ranger, a guy nearly walked right into one on the way in and I nearly walked right into it on the way out.

From there we had to make a choice. We wanted to make our way back north to explore some of the picturesque mountain towns on the Western Slope that we rarely got the chance to see. The two options on the table were Telluride and Ouray. We had a passing thought of trying to hit both, but the distance between the two and our short timeline was a little too prohibitive. They're incredibly close to each other as the crow flies, just on either side of a small mountain range, but to get there by road meant venturing hours out of our way.

We ultimately set our sights on Telluride, which did not fall short of our expectations. The town was nestled in a tight valley surrounded by imposing mountains. Shortly before we arrived we came over a pass and had to pull off to stare in awe at a pristine, sapphire blue lake. Once in town we grabbed a quick lunch at a Mexican restaurant then began exploring. A little German import shop caught our eye as it advertised in the window that the owner had three Bernese Mountain Dogs and frequently brought them to work with him. Crystal and I had just lost our dog that spring so we had to go say hi to the pups. There only happened to be one that day, and Crystal spent the entire time trying to make friends with him. He was similar to our previous dog, affable but standoffish around new people, so it took Crystal a while to gain his trust. Ray and I made small talk with the shop owner so that he wouldn't think we were just crazies off the street. We learned that he would be marching with all of his dogs in an Independence Day parade through town the following week. One of them would even be pulling a decorative cart to pay homage to their working dog heritage. I ended up buying one of the seminal works of literature on Bernese Mountain Dogs and the shop owner gave me a discount because we were, as he put it, friends of the breed.

Storm clouds were starting to gather at that point, so I made a quick stop in an outfitter to pick up a rain jacket because I hadn't brought anything waterproof. Undeterred by the pending storm, we caught the chair lift up to the top of the local ski slope. There wasn't any snow of course, but it was available for hiking. We wandered through the picturesque scenery for twenty or thirty minutes then decided we should set off for our next hotel. On our way back down I made note of a sign that helped identify undetonated explosives in the snow. The ski patrol used them to set off avalanches when the slopes were closed, but apparently some were duds and wouldn't explode until triggered by an unwitting skier.

While we were planning our trip Crystal had been looking up local things to do beyond the standard tourist sights. She discovered that Paonia held a cherry festival near the Fourth of July every year. We were going to check it out the next day, so we booked a room in nearby Delta at what turned out to be the nicest hotel of the whole vacation. The other nights were at large hotel chains whereas this was more of a mom and pop motel. It had a full kitchen, a walk out patio, and a whole lot of heart. It was a hidden jewel and we congratulated Crystal on finding it.

We had a quiet night ahead of us, so Ray sat down to research some of the area. We had seen two of Colorado's National Parks, and if he was right there were only four total in the state. Of course Ray was right. We had already seen the Great Sand Dunes and Mesa Verde, which left Rocky Mountain National Park and the Black Canyon of the Gunnison. Neither Crystal nor I had ever heard of that last one, but it turned out we were roughly thirty minutes away and the north side was partly on the route to Paonia. Since we were so close already we decided to make a point of seeing all the parks before we were done. In the morning we ate some boiled eggs and oatmeal at the hotel and hit the road.

We made it to the Black Canyon in short order and damn was I glad Ray brought it up. It wasn't as grand as the Grand Canyon of course, but it was still immense. While not that wide across it was vertigo-inducingly deep, and the rock face rising up from the surface of the river below was almost an obsidian black. It was incredible to behold. We spent about a half hour taking in the sights before heading out.

We pulled into Paonia about an hour later and applied our sunscreen much more carefully than we had at the Sand Dunes. By then the spots on my triceps were bright red and peeling. With our skin adequately screened we made our way to the Cherry Festival. I have always loved little events that show off the local color. The Boulder Creek Festival during Memorial Day weekend has been a staple of my life since I was in elementary school. Granted, it's a bit bizarre to throw a festival celebrating a creek, but it gives a sense of what's important to the community. We passed a number of cherry orchards on our way into town, so a cherry festival made sense to us.

There was a lot of standard festival fare. We chowed down on some finger food. Crystal reserved sixteen pounds of cherries that we would turn into jam and dried fruit later that summer. We were especially enthralled by the coal shoveling event. We watched for a solid twenty minutes as teams of two stood on either side of a cart and shoveled as much coal as possible into it from an enormous mound. The load was weighed after each heat and dumped back onto the ground for the next team. One guy was so adept he shoveled all the coal from his side then stepped around to help shovel his teammate's side. It was something to see.

We wrapped up our visit by eating some cherry ice cream at a local shop. It wasn't until we had finished ordering and begun to dig in that we learned the ice cream was all imported and none of the cherries were local. So much for small town charm. We hit the road and made our way northeast toward Glenwood Springs. We arrived with just enough time for a little dinner at a local brewery and a dip in the hot springs. I hadn't been to the springs since my trip to Utah with Dean and Alan nearly a decade before. It had been at least as long for Crystal and Ray as well, so we braved the crowds and ventured into the water.

We spent about a half hour wading around before an advisory came over the speaker warning everyone that lightning was striking in the area. They suggested we exit the pool and seek shelter, and pretty much everyone did including ourselves. With the lightning came pouring rain, so we stood in the locker room watching to see if the storm would let up and allow us to go back. After about fifteen minutes we were cold, wet, and shivering in the doorway, but unwilling to give up. The resort was closing soon, and we wanted one last dip before we left. We trotted out through the rain and jumped into the spring once again. I can't speak to how good of an idea that was, but having the cool water showering our heads while our bodies were warmed by the natural thermal activity below felt amazing. I was glad we'd gone back in.

We stayed until the staff kicked us out then we got some sleep at the hotel. In the morning we had a small breakfast at the hotel and set out bright and early. Ray had singled out one of the many white water rafting companies in town to give us a tour of the Colorado river. He and Crystal had rafted before, but this was going to be my first time. We suited up outside what looked like an old firehouse then ran through a general orientation. Basic stuff like what signals the guide would give us, how to position our bodies if we were thrown overboard, how to use the butt of the paddles to hook someone and pull them back in the raft. After all that was done we boarded a bus and drove east up I-70 to a good launch point.

The journey by raft was pleasant and offered a perspective on the area that I never got from the highway. That said, I could not have been happier to disembark when we finally reached our destination. Wedging myself in while still maintaining the ability to row meant I had to spend a good forty-five minutes torquing my back out of position. I slowly loosened up as we ate lunch at a little German place in town.

Once my spine was happier we charted a course north through Rocky Mountain National Park, thus completing our tour of every national park in Colorado. Sadly there wasn't much to do as we passed through. The storm from the night before had shifted up to that area, so the atmosphere was cold and wet. As if that wasn't discouraging enough, we were flagged down by a ranger just before we reached tree line and told to stay in our car because lightning had been spotted nearby. Without trees around we would be the tallest thing in the area, putting us at severe risk of being struck. We took in what views we could get through the car windows before making our way home to Boulder.

That was only the latest in a number of road trips I took with Ray. In the spring of 2012 it was time for him to bid farewell to Colorado and start a new adventure. He had graduated in 2011 and spent nearly a year looking for a job. That's why it was cause for celebration when he landed a position down in Phoenix, even if we were all sad to see him go. The company paid to ship all of his clothing and furnishings to his new apartment, which just left the matter of getting his car to Arizona. Nick, Crystal, and I volunteered to road trip down with him as a last hurrah.

The plan was to do the drive in two days and spend a third exploring Phoenix. We left a little before noon and had an uneventful drive to New Mexico. We made Santa Fe in time for a late lunch, and the sun was just starting to set as I took the driver's seat near Albuquerque. That made for some blinding moments as we traveled west along I-40. Some climbs were so steep and the sun was so low that I couldn't see anything other than the car immediately ahead of me. A couple hours after the sun set completely I handed the reins to Crystal for the last leg of the day. I had grown so accustomed to long haul road trips with just one other person in the car that it felt bizarre to only have one shift in a day.

In the morning we detoured north to the Grand Canyon. I'd never seen it before myself, so I was eager for the chance.

The approach was a bit tedious as the speed limit dropped and the road became shallow rolling hills with hardly any change in terrain. The four of us perked up once we finally arrived at the canyon though. I walked out on an observation platform and stared speechless at the landscape in front of me. The far rim was so distant the color appeared to be slightly bluer than normal, making the whole scene look as though it was painted on canvas. We took in the view for about twenty minutes before we decided we wanted to experience it, not just look at it, and began trekking down one of the foot trails. We only made it a few hundred yards into the canyon before we discovered patches of snow were still resisting the spring thaw. Some clung to shaded spots on the trail where they had partially melted then reformed over and over to create treacherous sheets of ice. None of us had any sort of crampons to create purchase, so we abandoned our misguided adventure and set off for Ray's new home.

We backtracked to Flagstaff then took I-17 south toward Phoenix. That drive was an experience unto itself. There was more than a mile of elevation difference between the two, and nearly two thousand feet of that dropped off in a single twenty-mile stretch from Arcosanti to Black Canyon City. Shortly thereafter the famed saguaro cactus began dotting the landscape. They appeared as perfectly straight cylinders towering as much as forty-five feet over the desert floor. Seeing our first was cause for excitement. Seeing the massive expanse of them as we neared Phoenix was cause for awe.

We arrived in Phoenix a little after nightfall and discovered just how massive the city was. It sprawled across the desert, consuming other cities like Tempe and Scottsdale in its gluttony. It was a very low city though. We could drive for miles without seeing a structure more than two stories tall. We traversed the great arterial highways that pumped millions of citizens throughout the area on our way to Ray's new apartment. The main office was closed by the time we pulled into the parking lot, but he'd gotten the key when he signed the lease a few weeks before. We dropped our suitcases inside and set out for some provisions. His furniture wasn't set to arrive until later that week, so he bought an air mattress that he generously let Crystal and I use during our stay. Nick was relegated to curling up on the floor. We had a small dinner, acutely aware that this would be our last evening together for quite some time, then bedded down at the apartment.

I never spent a colder night in the desert than that. We all froze our asses off in relative solitude, unwilling to confer with each other about how outrageously cold it was. After an hour or so I got fed up and actually inspected the thermostat only to discover it was turned off. I turned on the heat and nearly jumped at the immense rumbling that spewed from the HVAC system. Afraid I would wake up the whole household and assuming incorrectly that I was the only one so cold I turned it off and went back to bed.

We started the next day at a little breakfast joint Crystal and I had heard of. I had a meal of three breakfast sausages dipped in pancake batter and deep fried like corn dogs. The server brought my plate but told me to wait before digging in. He had brought an empty plate, which he proceeded to cover with maple syrup and hot sauce. I was to dip the breakfast dogs in that. In doing so I experienced new revelations about the universe. Ray ordered something called The Wolf Pack, which consisted of about two pounds of hash browns mixed with every breakfast meat known to man. I'm not sure what everyone else got. The rest of the world was dead to me as I began eating my breakfast dogs.

The rest of the day was spent shopping for furnishings and exploring the city. Before long it was time to pack up our things and head to the airport. Ray dropped us off and we said our sad goodbyes before catching a plane back to Denver. Little did I know that two years later, in the spring of 2014, I'd be flying back to Phoenix with Crystal to undo everything we had just done. By then Ray was eager to be rid of Phoenix. It wasn't just hot, it was hot all the time. The 120 degree days in the summer would have been tolerable except that the city got no reprieve from the heat. Even in the dead of night the mercury would push above ninety-five. Ray had no intention of suffering another Arizona summer.

While I was ecstatic to have him come back to Colorado, I was a little sorry to see him leave Phoenix. I'd grown fond of the city and I liked having a reason to visit. In 2013 I was between jobs and convinced Crystal to fly down and visit Ray for a week with me. The same plane ride in 2014 had a certain finality to it.

The apartment was all but bare when we arrived. It looked much as it had when we'd moved Ray in two years prior. We helped gather the few remaining belongings and hit the road the next day. Ray had bought a brand new Mazda 3 shortly after he arrived in Phoenix, so this trip was much more posh than our first journey.

We'd decided not to repeat our visit to the Grand Canyon and instead check out Monument Valley and the Four Corners area. It would again be a two day drive, and we spent the first night in a little hotel along US-163 just across the border in Utah. We pulled in at night on a little incline, unloaded our things, and fell asleep. The morning we woke to some of the most spectacular views I'd ever seen. Our hotel window overlooked Monument Valley itself, with massive rock formations rising a hundred feet or more above the desert. When we got outside we discovered the little incline that led us into the parking lot was the base of another massive rock face that loomed over the entirety of the hotel. We had no idea such majesty was lurking in the darkness as we made our approach the previous night.

We snagged a map of the area so we could identify each formation by name then eagerly piled into Ray's car and set off into the valley itself. Our little sedan bumped along the rocky path well enough given the people who built it never had this terrain in mind. We pulled over a few times to marvel at the scenic outlooks and mingle with dozens of tourists all clamoring to take the exact same photos. Time was getting away from us though, so we decided to turn back rather than continuing through the full loop around the valley.

We arrived at the Four Corners Monument later that afternoon and took the obligatory photos placing a limb in each state. We learned that, due to a surveying error decades before, the monument was not on the site of the four actual state corners. We paid that little detail no mind. It's not likely to move any time soon. In addition to the monument proper that's inlaid in the ground, there were booths arrayed all around for artists to sell jewelry and the like. There weren't many shops open that day, it was probably the off season so early in the year, but we mingled with the few artisans that were there. On the way out I made note of the fact that it's illegal to spread human ashes in the monument as cremation is seen as a desecration of the human body to the tribe that owns that land.

The rest of the drive was uneventful. The landscape became progressively snowier as we entered and traversed Colorado. It had been cold through much of our journey, we wore coats and hats as we explored Monument Valley, but now we began to see drifts piled up alongside the highway with wisps of frost threading through the lanes themselves. Denver was playing in the Super Bowl that evening against Seattle, which was a matchup doomed to be one of the most crushing defeats in my time following the team. To add insult to injury, the only way we could follow the game was to stream it from a radio station based in Seattle. Every interception Denver threw was greeted with ecstatic cheers from the announcers. We eventually had to turn the whole debacle off.

I drove the last leg of the trip. While we were stopped to get gas Ray and I decided to bet on how long it would take to get back to my house. Why Ray would compete with me when I had the wheel was a little baffling. Ultimately we pulled into my driveway exactly when I predicted we would, right down to the second. I only rubbed it in his face a little. In any case, this time we said much less sad goodbyes as Ray was back and we had many more journeys in store for us.

That was the thing about Ray, he was always up for a good adventure. I roomed with him multiple times throughout college precisely for that reason. He was one of my closest friends and a constant companion in my adolescence. Perhaps our first road bound adventure came our Junior year of high school. My cousin needed to borrow The Icebox for his own adventure down to South Padre, so I handed him the keys and took his Honda Prelude for a week. It was a pretty crappy car all told, but anything sleeker than a cube and faster than a tortoise seemed like a proper sports car to me. The night we made the switch I headed over to Dean's basement to see who was around from the normal crew. There were a lot of folks milling about doing nothing in particular, so when I suggested we go cruising about four of them jumped at the idea. This was in spite of the fact that a Prelude was a glorified two seater. How three of those guys squeezed into the back I'll never know, but they did and we were off.

We headed north on US-36 to Lyons because it was close and there weren't typically cops skulking about in the evening. I still took it pretty easy. We just cruised up and down the highway for an hour then headed back to town. The night was getting late so I was dropping folks off at their respective homes. Soon it was just Mikko, Ray, and myself in the car. Mikko lived up along 4th street around the point where the regular neighborhoods petered out and multi-million dollar foothills mansions began. I dropped him off then drove north on 4th with Ray until we came to one of the steeper cross streets. I gave the car just enough gas to make it through the intersection and threw it into neutral. I wasn't so bold as to try catching air like Dean allegedly had, but it was enough to get us going at a good clip. We just about doubled the speed limit before I had to slam the brakes to keep from running the stop sign at the bottom of the hill.

Three or four blocks later I turned onto Broadway and was immediately caught by flashing lights in my rearview. I was sure he had seen me blasting down the hill and was pulling me over for that. The cop came to my window and asked for my license, registration, and insurance before interrogating us about what we were doing in the area. I told him we had just dropped my friend off and were heading home ourselves as I fumbled for my credentials. I had the license and registration easy enough, but the insurance was another matter. Between the center console and the glovebox my cousin had about eight different insurance cards, all of which were expired. While I was digging through every last nook and cranny the cop circled around the vehicle, scanning every surface with his flashlight. He asked Ray for his license and ran a check on both of us. Fortunately he ignored the fact that I couldn't find a valid proof of insurance to save my life.

The background check came back clean of course, and he returned our licenses to us. At that point he told us that someone had just reported a hit and run in the area. Since he couldn't find any signs of damage on our car he let us go. No mention of our recent cruise down the foothills. I was glad to put distance between him and us as I got Ray home.

As the week drew to a close I had an ache for one last blast of speed in the Prelude. I called Ray up because he was always willing to enable my bad decisions. He didn't disappoint me that night. I picked him up and headed toward the reservoir. The byways in that area had always provided us with the cover we needed for illegitimate activities. Admittedly, the dirt roads were a bad choice for tests of speed, but I was young and foolish. I set my sights on one particular stretch that was just about a mile long and bounded by T-junctions on either side. In my head, my plan had all the makings of a Hollywood chase scene. I would build up speed approaching the intersection at one end of the stretch, pull a fast U-turn with the handbrake, burnout going the opposite direction, then try to hit a hundred mph before coming to the intersection at the other end.

After a couple practice runs I was feeling confident in my ability to make the turn without sending us careening into a ditch. From there I worked out the logistics of the burnout, figuring out if I would get more acceleration dropping down to first or riding the momentum straight into second. Finally I attempted it in earnest, but a couple poor shifts meant I only got up to about seventy-five mph before I had to hit the brakes.

By that time I had done maybe a dozen turns and driven the length of the runway twice, so I was worried the households in the area were aware of our presence. I had an itch for speed that I hadn't yet scratched though, so I needed to do one last run. For my final run I did a solid forty all the way back into the handbrake turn. I nearly spun out from all the speed, but I whipped the tail back in line and took off as hard as I could. I rode each gear until I was up to four or five thousand RPM, trying to wring every last ounce of acceleration out of the transmission. The speedometer shot to sixty before I knew it, then climbed steadily to seventy. I could see glints of light off the stop sign in the distance. Eighty. The speedometer started to slow. Ninety. Damn a mile could go by quick. Ninety-five. The sign stood imperiously just a few hundred yards ahead. Ninety-seven. Ninety-eight. Ninety-nine. The moment I hit hundred I laid on the brake as hard as I could without locking up. The world finally expanded back to full view. There was more to life than a speedometer and a stop sign. There was the road in front of me, the car all around me, and Ray next to me, steadfast through the entire adventure.

I pulled to a stop three feet from the road ahead, and it would have been impossible for me to stop any sooner. There it was, a hundred mph and back in less than a mile. I calmly undid my seat belt, stepped from the car, and screamed. A primal, unwavering, wordless scream until I'd emptied my lungs of all air. When I stepped back in the car Ray turned to me and laughed. He told me that he thought I was about to vomit on the road. I smiled at him and we drove home.

Truth be told there was very little I could do that would ever faze Ray. He eagerly participated in all of my grandiose plans and patiently suffered my harebrained schemes. I could tell a thousand stories of nights like that one and they would all end the same. He never wavered in his friendship. He stood by me for all the years I ran wild trying to figure out who I was, and he gave me the support I needed to forge my own identity.

5

In the summer of 2010 Crystal and I had the insane idea to road trip all the way to the East Coast. I was itching to get back to New York ever since my trip with Dean, and Boston had always held a certain appeal. It didn't hurt that we had friends in both cities that could give us a bed and show us around. On paper it sounded perfect. The ridiculousness came from the fact that we wanted to do it in a single week. We'd leave Denver on a Saturday and arrive in Boston that Sunday. The following weekend we'd leave New York on Saturday and arrive back in Denver on Sunday. That put us at nearly 2,000 miles of driving each way. Factor in bathroom breaks and lunch and we were looking at two consecutive days of driving seventeen hours. That didn't sound so bad until we left Denver at 6:00 AM, hit South Bend, Indiana at midnight, crawled into bed at the hotel around 1:00 AM, got up at 6:00 AM, and did it all again. That would have been hard enough with three people in the car when we could have rotated through naps the entire trip. As it was just the two of us, the passenger felt obligated to stay awake nearly the whole time so that the driver wouldn't fall asleep at the wheel.

The first day was pretty uneventful. We retraced the same tracks I'd taken with my family so many times before when we'd travel to Madison, Wisconsin, in the summers. The only difference being that we didn't cut north after hitting Des Moines. We kept going straight on through to Illinois and Indiana. That was about when we began our love affair with Steak 'n Shake. It had been a favorite with Crystal during her own family road trips to see her grandmother. I had never had it before, but once I took my first bite I couldn't stop. Over the course of the nine day trip we would probably stop at five Steak 'n Shakes across the country, sometimes hitting multiple in a single day.

On the second day of travel we got tired of tollways real quick. It would have cost us about fifteen dollars just to drive through Ohio, so we cut up to OH-2 along Lake Erie when we had the chance. We spent our day trying to figure out the best route to keep both our travel time and toll costs as low as possible. By the time we were rolling through Massachusetts that night we couldn't care anymore. A full day and a half in the car with hardly any sleep had taken its own sort of toll on us, and we were pretty much willing to pay whatever it cost to shorten our trip.

I was behind the wheel for the last leg of the journey, strung out and half-delirious. We nearly missed our exit and the mere thought of spending one more minute in the car than necessary sent me into a state of raving madness. I started half-shouting, half-pleading to Crystal, "You have to help me! You have to help me!" I'm not sure now if I meant help with directions or help just surviving the night. The two were intertwined in my mind at the time. We made it through the city streets and arrived at Emma's apartment not too long after that, but we quickly discovered parking was a goddamn mess in her neighborhood. We circled the block twice trying to figure out if there was anywhere on the street we could leave our car. At last we just drove up on an unpaved embankment that seemed as good a place as any and rang Emma to come fetch our sorry party. Once again the clock was pushing midnight. Emma had a couple sleeping bags she rolled out on the floor for us and they felt like manna from heaven for our road weary bones.

In the morning we briefly chatted with her roommates as they were on their way out the door. It was Monday and Emma had taken a few days off work to spend with us, but her roommates had not. Once they left she explained the insanity that was her apartment's parking situation. They had a private lot, but it was not much wider than a typical alleyway. There were no lines drawn and no illusion that we could actually navigate our car through it when it was full. Cars were parked two abreast to accommodate all of the tenants, so the social convention was that everyone left a note on their dashboard with their name and phone number. If my car was blocked in I would call the owner of the other car, hope they answered, and have them move out of my way. If there was more than one car blocking me in, I better start dialing early.

None of that mattered though. We had arrived and it was two and a half days before we needed to use the car again. We were glad to be rid of the headache of driving, and we set off on our whirlwind tour of Boston. If there's one thing that can be said about Emma's hospitality it's that she was a hell of a tour guide. Even though we'd only given her a couple weeks notice she already knew everything she wanted to show us. We walked through the brownstones then stopped at the wharf for lunch. We walked along a pier about ten feet above the waters of the Atlantic, and I was a bit sad that I couldn't dip my feet in the water. The prior year I had been with Will on the opposite end of the country, standing in the waters of the Pacific, when he remarked that he had finally set foot in every major body of water that surrounded the country. I was hopeful that I could one day replicate his feat, but there would be no opportunity to touch the Atlantic on this trip. In fact, it would be another seven years before I waded into the vast eastern ocean and completed my circuit.

We continued our tour of Boston and briefly followed the red line that runs through a number of important Revolutionary War sites in the city. We gave a passing nod to our forebears as time was fleeting and instead used the line as a means to our own ends. Emma knew of a fantastic place a little off the path that specialized in cannolis. Crystal and I were all for the excursion though nothing could have prepared us for what we were to find when we reached our destination. The shop itself wasn't that big, maybe the size of a two bedroom apartment, but every wall was lined with display cases devoted to cannolis. It was more than my sleep deprived brain could handle. I spent about twenty minutes walking back and forth like a lunatic examining every possible option, reading the additional flavors on the boards hanging behind the counters, and staring with wonder at how employees bundled each order. They carefully laid the cannoli in a box to go, reached for one of many giant spools of string hanging from the ceiling, and feverishly wrapped the package a dozen times or more before tying it off in a neat bow.

At last I settled on a peanut butter cannoli thinking that a hint of peanut butter in the cannoli filling would yield a delectable result. Crystal, Emma, and I all placed our orders together then continued whatever conversation we were having. The attendant packed up our little parcel and we headed for home. A half hour later we arrived back at Emma's apartment and unpacked our treats. It was at this point I finally looked upon my peanut butter cannoli with abject horror. It was not the delectable blend of peanut butter, ricotta, and powdered sugar that I had anticipated. Instead, I discovered two heaping scoops of standard, off-the-shelf peanut butter piped into a cannoli shell. No subtlety, no craftsmanship, no delectable culinary arts. It looked and tasted like a dog treat. Enraged, I exclaimed as much while Emma and Crystal nearly died laughing. I couldn't finish the thing.

The rest of the evening was spent hanging around Emma's apartment. She told us about a recent trip to Vegas with a bunch of her guy friends. She paid special attention to one particular night when they all went to a strip club together. The group soon noticed a pattern in which each dancer that approached them would single out a guy, begin working him over, but invariably strike up a conversation with Emma. So she spent her night chatting with the entertainment while the guys spent their night being entertained.

I was glad for our quiet evening catching up with Emma. She had a certain moxie and sardonic wit that always made me laugh. I hated her a little when she announced she would be leaving for Boston after high school. Throughout college I would try goading her to move back to Boulder, but it never worked. She went east to pursue a career in law, worked at a firm for a couple years, hated it, quit, and started a new life as a teacher at an inner-city school. Emma always did what was right by her, no matter how difficult. I missed her when she left, but truth be told I always admired her intrepid spirit.

The next day was another bit of walking as we trekked over to the Sam Adams brewery. There was a rail line that would have cut our travel time in half, but it was affectionately known as The Murder Line by the locals, so we hoofed it instead. Crystal was forbidden to drink while on the premises as she was just twenty at the time. That was no surprise, but we were all annoyed that they wouldn't even let her have the commemorative glass everyone else got for free. The walk through the brewery was relatively short, and we were soon ushered into the large communal tasting room. This seemed like the big draw of the tour. We sat at three great tables and bartenders sent pitchers down the line. Emma and I drank heartily with our commemorative glasses while Crystal could only look on and steal an occasional whiff of the beers.

In the morning we started making arrangements to leave town. Our car was only slightly buried in the abysmal parking lot of Emma's apartment. There was a single car between us and the open road. We were keen to get out before rush hour, so we called the girl blocking us before breakfast. No answer. We talked for a bit and called again. No answer. We waited a half hour and called again. No answer. All together we were held up until about 2:00 PM. At that point we were helpless to avoid a New York City rush hour. What demon dreamt up the interstate system in that city? With so many thoroughfares packed bumper to bumper, it might take twenty minutes to change lanes. That is, if anyone had any self-preservation whatsoever. The rubber mats hanging off the trunk of every third car made me think that wasn't such a concern. From what I could tell, it wouldn't prevent any actual damage. It had a large smooth area that would imprint the license plate so the driver could take the hit, continue along his merry way, then report the offense later.

The whole debacle made me insane, but no matter. I had finally figured out the route. I positioned myself in exactly the correct lane to get off at our last exit of the day. We carried along, slow but steady. About a quarter mile from the end of our journey the cars ahead of me started merging to other lanes. I figured that would just clear more space for me. It wasn't until we were an eighth of a mile from the exit that I finally discovered the reason everyone was getting over. A construction sign was sitting in the middle of my lane. No apparent reason at all except to snap the last nerve I had, which it did. Something broke in me that instant. I was done. I was just done. I wouldn't get over again. I wasn't trying to weave my way through traffic even once more. It was 6:00 PM and I figured traffic would die down in an hour or two. I would just wait it out. No problem.

Just as I chose the path of inaction, a miracle happened. The car behind me forced its way over then waved me in. Maybe there was some unspoken bond between us that day as we both had Colorado plates. Maybe it was just a mistake on his part. Who knows. I couldn't care less at that point. We were finally in Walt's neighborhood and done with the car once more. We made our way up to his apartment. He was moving in and prepping for the arrival of his new roommate, another friend of ours from Boulder. He had set up a little guest room, though it was more a guest closet. It didn't matter. Just having our own space after sleeping on the floor in Emma's living room was a nice step up.

We were exhausted from our journey so we didn't do much our first night in town. Walt unpacked a box of his art then explained the principle behind a makeshift still he was concocting out of a tea kettle and a few yards of pliable copper tubing. He was a man of boundless ingenuity. We played a game of Scrabble on his living room floor. We examined a deck of drink cards he was designing. The idea was to create a set of easily recognizable icons to represent different alcohols and mixers, plus what glass to properly serve the drink in, then assemble a full deck of 52 recipes.

Eventually we grew hungry, and Walt had just the place in mind. About six blocks down the road was a big, open air beer garden. There was a mild line in front of the door as a bouncer was checking IDs. We took our place and slowly advanced forward as people continued to file in behind us. Apparently the beer garden was the place to be that night. We weren't exactly sure what would happen once we made it to the door with Crystal underage, but we were game to find out. We finally reached the bouncer who was a slender old man. Walt and I handed him our driver's licenses and he nodded us through. Then Crystal handed hers to him. He took a good long look directly at it, examining it all over, before he turned his head away, handed it back, and muttered something under his breath like, "Works for me." Crystal grabbed her license and took a tentative step into the garden with a sidelong look at the bouncer. When he gave no reaction she stepped lively and we made a beeline for a table.

To this day we have no idea what the hell he said but we were glad for his complacency. We ordered a giant sampler plate that had about three pounds of meat plus sauerkraut and fries for the three of us to share. We grabbed a few beers, then Walt went and got a round of fernet and Coke. It was the first and only time I ever enjoyed fernet. Something about how they mixed it at the beer garden was cool and refreshing. Just what we needed on a hot summer night. Every fernet I've had since has just tasted like grass clippings. As we were just finishing our drinks we noticed a new bouncer make two passes by our table in quick succession, and we decided we didn't want to press our luck with a third. We paid our tab and got out before he had a mind to check our IDs again.

The next day we hopped the train to Manhattan. The sight of Walt on a subway made me happy. Big cities suited him well. It was nothing intrinsic to him or the city itself. Really, it was the fact that Walt was the worst driver I have ever seen in my life, and any city that precluded the need for a car was ideal for him. I've lost count of all the harrowing experiences I've had in a car with Walt. I came of age with a crowd of guys that drove big cars and drove them hard. We would doggedly pace each other across dirt roads deep in the mountains with nothing but a giant pair of brass balls telling us that we were not about to slide right off the embankment into a stand of aspens. Walt was not one of those young men though, and that's not the sort of harrowing adventure I'm referring to.

A favorite story of Walt's driving career came to me from him and him alone, so take it with a grain of salt. He was out for an evening drive while listening to his favorite classical arrangements. That was when an officer of the law decided to pull him over for suspicion of general adolescent tomfoolery.

The cop sauntered up to Walt's door and began accosting him, claiming he reeked of alcohol. Walt had not had a single drop to drink that evening and was adamantly explaining as much. Eventually the cop simply demanded license and registration, but as Walt reached for his wallet he somehow tripped the recline lever on his seat and dropped out of sight. What's more, his foot slipped off the brake and the car, that was inexplicably still in gear, began a creeping getaway down the street. Thus began the slowest police chase in the history of Boulder as the cop walked alongside a seemingly driverless car shouting for it to stop while it dispassionately blasted Tchaikovsky in response.

Again, I've never corroborated this story, but given my own experiences with the man I'm inclined to believe it. Walt approached driving the way Al Capone approached tax law. Sure there were rules, but he had neither the time nor the patience to abide by them. He got where he was going and let everyone else sweat the details. Proper traffic decorum was not becoming of a man of his stature.

Back to the story at hand though. Walt had been earning extra cash leading tours through the city, and he was in prime fashion when it came time to take us on a walking tour of the city. We headed south past Wall St, the Charging Bull, and on to Battery Park. After that it was back up north to wander Strand Book Store where I picked up a CD pressing of Jack Kerouac's *Doctor Sax and the Great World Snake*. I thought it was an extraordinary find. Once we finished our exploration of Strand, we insisted that Walt venture with us to a nearby burger joint coincidentally named Stand. We'd heard of them in context of their toasted marshmallow milkshake in which a standard vanilla milkshake was infused with toasted marshmallow fluff and topped with an actual marshmallow that had been viciously assaulted with a brûlée torch. We each got one along with a burger, then ordered another shake to share for the road. It was time to get back to the apartment after all, so we took the train to Astoria and got some rest.

The next day we did some more exploring about the city. We went up to Central Park then walked about the Met. We went up to the roof and took in the sights of the city. Crystal got yelled at by a security guard who thought she was touching art. I guess it's all a matter of perspective in an art museum. We left and headed to Times Square where we sat on a giant set of illuminated stairs and were dazzled by all the lights. Once we had our fill Walt insisted on taking us to the High Line Park.

The first section of the park had just opened the prior year. It was originally a set of elevated train tracks built directly through numerous buildings and was used to ship goods throughout the city. The rail line was decommissioned in 1980 and the whole track was nearly torn down shortly thereafter. Instead a group successfully lobbied for it to be preserved and turned into a city park suspended above the streets. The whole thing was a series of boardwalks littered with cultivated landscapes. Many of the tenants situated along the park had embraced the idea as well. Nearby balconies were brightly decorated, and many tenants would sip a drink while conversing with park goers. Walt told us that some would even put on short theatrical performances for passers by. It was wonderful, but we had a long journey ahead of us the next day. We walked the length of the park then made our way back to Walt's apartment. That would be the last night I spent in New York for nearly six years.

In the morning we said our goodbyes and hit the road as quickly as we could. The agony of the drive ahead was still fresh in our minds from the prior weekend. We decided to see more of the nation rather than retracing our same route back. That meant heading southeast through New Jersey on a trajectory toward I-70. Shortly over the border we stopped to get gas. I began pumping at the station only to discover I had grievously insulted the attendant working there. He came out and waved me away with a grunt. I was puzzled at first then realized New Jersey was one of the few states left that did not allow individuals to pump their own gas. Little did I know at that moment Liam, Ray, and Nick were stranded by the same situation on the opposite end of the country. They had to spend the night in a gas station parking lot in Oregon waiting for the attendant to arrive the next morning and fill them up.

Fortunately for Crystal and I, the experience amounted to little more than an inconvenience, and we continued on the way. We made a note that the trip from New York to Denver was slightly shorter than the trip from Denver to Boston. I was glad of that for no other reason than I wanted to be off the road as soon as possible. Crystal had other ideas. She had heard tell of Hershey, Pennsylvania, the home of the famed Hershey candy company. I figured it would be a basic factory with nothing much to see, and I argued that we should pass it by. Crystal's persistence won out. It was only fifteen minutes or so off the interstate anyway, so we decided to stop. When we arrived I discovered I could not have been more wrong in my assumptions.

Perhaps a humble factory stood somewhere on the property, but Hersheypark was a full, candy-themed amusement park complete with a tram to take guests throughout the grounds.

The weight of the 1,600 some miles still ahead of us kept us from exploring the park to its fullest. We instead looked for the nearest feature that would make us feel the excursion had been worth it. We found a brand new attraction that was set to officially open in a few days, but they were allowing early, beta-test access to ensure everything was running smoothly. We took it as a sign that our travel so perfectly lined up with their schedule and stepped up to give it a try. It turned out to be a Wonka-esque attraction in which attendees designed their very own candy bar, packaging included. We donned hairnets and lab coats then stepped up to touchscreens where we selected candy fillings for our chocolate bar. From there we went to a massive, whimsical machine where we threw a grand lever to begin the production of our candy bar. That sent the candy bar base, which was a large chocolate bar with high sides and a hollowed out interior reminiscent of a barge, floating down the conveyor belt. The mechanism was encased in plexiglass, so we could observe the entire process but not interfere. Above the belt were numerous hoppers containing the various candy fillings that would be dispensed as the base passed underneath. I watched as my bar was filled to the brim then sealed with a layer of flowing chocolate.

At that point the bar was tagged and removed from the line to cool. While waiting we were encouraged to create a custom label for our candy bar, which amounted to arranging clip art on a background of our choosing. The label was then printed on the spot and wrapped around a metal box that contained the chocolate bar I had designed. At fifteen dollars a pop it was without question the most expensive candy bar I had ever purchased, but the whole experience was good for a lark. I left satisfied with our excursion in Pennsylvania.

From there we traversed the great Appalachian Mountains for the last time and continued our journey west. We had mostly been navigating by atlas that trip, but I decided to pull up directions on my phone to make sure we didn't make a wrong turn as the hours dragged on. At the time I decidedly did not have a smartphone, but I did have a GPS connection and I dropped a few dollars on a navigation app. We soon turned it off because it insisted that we needed to take every exit we came to, then subsequently merge back onto the highway.

The rest of the trip along I-70 was smooth enough. Traveling through the relatively tiny eastern states had a disorienting effect that made me feel like we were making more progress than we actually were. We would set foot in nine states that weekend, and we had passed through six before our journey was even half over. On Sunday we found ourselves passing Junction City, Kansas, headed west on I-70, the same route I had taken with Sterling and Liam in 2006. I couldn't decide which was worse: driving through at 4:30 PM as the last leg of a nearly thirty-hour trip from the East Coast, or driving through at 1:30 AM as the last leg of a fifteen-hour trip. In any case we were back in Colorado soon enough, and a few hours after that we arrived at Crystal's townhome in Denver. Crystal spent the last hundred miles of the trip describing the latest book she was reading in exact detail. This was a tactic we used to keep each other awake on long drives.

The next day turned into a whole debacle as I tried and failed to get back to work. If I had known it would be a bust anyway I would have much rather spent the extra time with Emma and Walt. Oh well, I would be back again anyway. The cities across America are like great magnetic poles, and the interstates between are fields drawing me ever forward. The further I travel from one the more I'm attracted to another, and New York pulls harder than any of them. Everyone is drawn there sooner or later.

The following years would see me in New York a half dozen times or more. A large contingent of friends even descended on the city for Walt's wedding in 2016. We spent a weekend exploring Brooklyn's bar scene, getting yelled at by bouncers at a deli, discovering that Crystal and I would never get our beloved toasted marshmallow shakes again, and of course catching up with Walt and his soon to be husband until the wee hours of the morning. Walt reprised his role as tour guide as he led a contingent of about forty of us on a meandering walk through Carroll Gardens. Even in the face of his impending nuptials he was as gregarious as ever.

That was the secret all along: a city alone could only exert so much force. The people were always the real draw. I've gone months without seeing certain friends, sometimes without even talking to them, but when we got together again it was like we never missed a beat. Dean had it right, we were all one another's roots, and that meant something. My friendships with Emma and Walt persisted throughout the years and across the miles, so I always felt the pull to the great cities in the east.

6

By the spring of 2009 the staff at the bowling alley had turned over. Eddie, Logan, Sheila, and just about everyone else had graduated. I was part of the new guard that was managing the place along with Will and Jake, so we had a little sway when we decided we wanted to take a couple weeks off for some grand West Coast trip. We had intended to set off on May 18th, but we postponed it a day when Will's friend Kelly flew in from New Orleans for a quick visit.

I woke up at 6:00 AM on the morning of the 19th raring to go and figuring Will and Jake were too. Trouble was, we hadn't made any firm plans for our departure. I dialed up Will who was very groggy on the other end of the line. He thought we would leave around noon. He was game to get going sooner though. I headed over to his place to load my bags into his Honda Civic. It was in the best shape for the drive and Will had just acquired a new GPS device that he was eager to try out. It was Magellan brand, so we referred to it as M for the entire trip as a nod to our favorite Bond films. I figured we'd be hearing from Jake at any time, so I sat around Will's place while he packed his things. As it turned out, Jake didn't even wake up until we finally called him at 1:00 in the afternoon. To Jake's merit, he got his gear together pretty quick and we hit the road by three.

We cut between two ominous thunderstorms along I-80 and made it to Utah without incident. Our first stop was Park City where we bunked in the camper of a family Jake knew. We drank some mead I had brewed earlier that month and played Oregon Trail II attempting to recreate our journey as settlers in the 1800s. Jake died in two minutes when he fell through the ice fording a river, so we scratched that game and started over. The second game we were much more prepared, at least mentally. We still only equipped our settler party with a few hundred pounds of bacon and a rifle. We would continue updating our game to match our actual progress throughout the trip. I'm happy to say our virtual selves made it safe and sound to Sacramento.

We contemplated staying a second night in Park City. The landscape was beautiful. Marv, the patriarch of our host family, was extremely nice to us. However, as the day drew on it became apparent that he didn't want us anywhere near his daughters. They weren't really interested either, so we shoved off. Jake had forgotten a toothbrush and a few other basics in his haste to pack, so we hit up a convenience store to grab what he needed then continued our journey west. Our next destination was Weed, California, to spend a few nights with Jake's grandparents.

I had come down with a cold the morning we left Colorado, and it had gotten progressively worse over night. As a result, my left ear wouldn't pressurize for all of Utah, nor any time until we were through Nevada. During the day my head would feel like it was slowly being packed with cotton and there was nothing I could do to alleviate the pain. Overnight my sinuses would slowly acclimate and achieve equilibrium, but the following day would inevitably bring more elevation change and start the whole ordeal over. For those days I did whatever I could to shirk my driving responsibilities so I could sit in the back and wallow in my own misery.

I'm getting ahead of myself though. We arrived at the massive expanse of nothing that is the Bonneville Salt Flats a few hours past Park City. We stopped at a rest stop and both Jake and I felt compelled to lick the ground to be sure that it was, in fact, salt. We ventured a few yards into the flats before turning back. It was like walking on a field of hard packed snow. It crunched under our feet and stuck incessantly to our shoes. We decided to take a brick with us, perhaps to salt the rim of a margarita with authentic Salt Flats salt.

I mused that a man could make a killing out there selling salt to unwitting tourists. Little clumps packaged in classy jars, cork and all. Bloated, middle aged women would waste precious road time ogling the wares, commenting "Oo, think how good this would look in our kitchen dinette!" Meanwhile their husbands would impatiently eye their watches, wanting nothing more than to get to Reno and drop a dime at the blackjack tables. How sweet that gin and tonic would taste as he made eyes at the cute waitress. Of course his wife would pay him no mind and instead turn to their son to ask if he would like a jar. With his interest piqued he would nod his head yes and she would snap up two jars, one for herself, and the salesman would shine his slick smile as they drove out of sight, content having gotten away with murder.

Thirty yards away from the road was a man in what I could only describe as a sail car that was immobilized for lack of wind. We decided to leave. Jake got a call from his mother as we were crossing the halfway point in Nevada. She had found a room for us in Reno for just fifty dollars, so we decided we should pull off for the night. It was already getting dark and according to M we still had many miles before we reached Weed. We hadn't left Park City until around 3:30 PM as Jake had wanted to perform for Marv and the family, which meant waiting until everyone was home from work.

We rolled into the Eldorado Hotel around 10:00 PM, took a shot of rum in our room, then hit the gaming floor. We really just wanted a few "free" drinks, so we sat down at the penny slots and blew a couple bucks. After having no luck with that we rethought our game plan. We posted up at the five cent video poker machines right next to the bar and pounded away for an hour and a half. Three Jack and Cokes later we headed back to the room. I had spent five dollars on slots and three for tip. Jake was down about twenty. Will had periodic bursts of luck but ended the night down. We called it and went to bed with California at our fingertips.

The next day we decided to bum around Reno for a few hours. We started off with a quick dip in the pool followed by lunch at the buffet where a portly woman thrust her presence upon us. We made small talk with her and learned that the USBC Women's Championship was in town at a place called the National Bowling Stadium. We had to go.

The National Bowling Stadium was everything the name suggested. It had nearly eighty lanes, enough to house the most prestigious bowling competitions. Looking down on the lanes was stadium seating that could hold around a thousand spectators. There were fewer than fifty of us in attendance that day, but Will, Jake, and I sat and watched the spectacle until most of the games had finished. Being employees of a bowling alley ourselves we were extremely intrigued by the self-driving lane cleaner they wheeled out after the event.

Once we had our fill of Reno we again set off for Weed. We were stopped at the border by a couple highway patrolmen who were checking all cars for fruits or vegetables. We had no such cargo, so we were waved through. Shortly thereafter we pulled off as we discovered a singular tree in the desert that was covered with dozens of pairs of shoes. It was clearly a local landmark and we wished we had some spare footwear to contribute to the monument. Instead I settled for writing our initials in a heart with a marker on one of the branches.

Our trip through Northern California was uneventful. The terrain became progressively more mountainous. Before long we found ourselves at the base of Mount Shasta where the town was located. We passed an absolutely glorious hill on the road in. I mentioned to Will and Jake that I had a strong compulsion to hike it. Little did I know such a feat would come in time.

We arrived at our destination and met Jake's step-grandma Cheryl. She showed us to our room while Grandpa James was in the shower. I should say she showed us to our rooms as they had set aside one room for each of us. Much to her befuddlement though, we told her we'd rather just all bunk in a single king bed in one room. Jake and Will had shared a twin bed in Marv's camper two nights prior, so even a single king was an upgrade.

Once we had dropped our bags in the room I couldn't help but gawk at Grandpa James' bookcase in the hallway. Gorgeous leather bound copies of The Canterbury Tales, the Iliad, the Odyssey, and other magnificent works. I was awestruck and Grandpa James caught me ogling it. In his day he had been a neurosurgeon in Kansas before serving as a medical officer in the Navy. He was an illustrious and well-read man. He gave us the grand tour of the house. We strolled around his garden and he told us about their recent bear trouble. We chatted with Cheryl awhile as she hand-fried corn tortillas into shells for a taco dinner. We ate to our hearts' content and went to bed. So ended the evening of May 21st.

On Friday morning we were awakened by a knocking at the door, which was an unexpected turn of events. All of us had decided over dinner to set out early in the morning for Black Butte, the hill I so longed for on the way in, so we all agreed to set our alarms for 6:00 AM. When the knock came at 6:50 we knew something had gone awry. We pulled ourselves together as quick as possible and managed to get out by 7:00. The path up Black Butte was stunning. It snaked back and forth up the slope with tight switchbacks every few hundred feet. Huge areas were covered with rocks left from slides in years past. We weaved our way through them as we slowly progressed upward. Grandpa James told us that the local high school students had a tradition of trying to hike a straight line to the top of the butte each year. We examined the ungroomed slope and tried to imagine how that was possible.

Once we made it to the summit Grandpa James stood back and let our experience unfold. First we discovered a square foundation about ten feet by ten feet. In this foundation was a large yellow smiley face painted on a rock. Under the smiley face painted on the rock in the foundation was a plastic container. In the container under the smiley face painted on the rock in the foundation were notes of remembrance from all who reached the summit. I pulled out a receipt from some recent purchase and we wrote our names and our journey and that we had come this long trek by way of 756 pounds of bacon as an ode to our virtual selves. Once we were done, Grandpa James reminisced about scattering his first wife's ashes there. Jake's dad had the honor of scattering them only to have them blow right back in his face. We made our way down and had breakfast back at Grandpa James' home.

After a filling meal we set off to a memorial statue garden, one of the many philanthropic projects that Grandpa James benefacted. An artist by the name of Elias lived on site in a tiny one-room shack that doubled as his workshop. He had been at it for years and had littered it with a great deal of memorabilia, mostly from his days in the Marines. The board members that supported the garden had recently decided the artist had suffered enough for his work and sought support to build him a nice log cabin where he could live. That way he could use the shack as his dedicated workshop. When no support came, the board, being mostly comprised of veterans themselves, decided to build it themselves. It was almost complete, so we took the tour while we waited for Elias to get back from some touchup work he was doing on the grounds. When he did arrive he was carrying a guitar that was about as old as me, and Jake set to jamming with it. Elias seemed to get a soulful kick out of the selections Jake had prepared. We visited for a bit longer before hitting the road. Grandpa James had more to show us in the area.

Will and I were completely exhausted so we slept in the car as we drove to Captain Jack's Stronghold. Grandpa James had given us a book to read up on it the night before, but we had gone to bed without doing our homework. Elias let us borrow *Bury My Heart at Wounded Knee*, so Jake read that along the way. Apparently Captain Jack, at least that was the name the white settlers called him, was a peaceful leader of the Modoc tribe. He allowed settlers to come to his land without asking anything in return. However, tensions grew as more and more came. Eventually resources became scarce so Captain Jack and the others began taking food and livestock from the settlers. They only took enough to survive, and most settlers were fine with it, considering it to be just a tax on their land. Others were outraged though and demanded the government intervene.

After a series of unfortunate events the Modocs moved to a reservation already inhabited by another tribe. Soon though they discovered the government had lied about the conditions and the support the Modocs would receive, so they decided to return to their land. After some more incidents, the Modocs moved into the lava rocks near a lake and the government got pissed. They laid siege to the lava fields where 150 Modocs were holding out, but to no avail. The landscape of the area was easily defended and the Modocs held the land for five months before the army finally cut off their water supply and ended the Modocs' resistance.

We had lunch there and hiked along a trail that weaved through the stronghold. It was no longer near the lake. The lake was drained some decades ago to create farmland and was a fraction of its former size. We had left M back at the house, so it wasn't until we were on our way back and were stopped by border patrol again asking if we had foreign fruits or vegetables that we learned we had actually crossed into Oregon at some point in the drive.

After the events of the day we decided it was high time for a beer. Well, it wasn't so much a group decision as Grandpa James telling us we were going to get a beer. Who were we to argue? It wasn't until we arrived at the Mt. Shasta Brewing Company that Will and Jake realized they didn't have their IDs. We had to make a quick stop back home then returned to the brewery as Grandpa James insisted on the excursion.

We decided to do the full sample of their lineup. There were six in all with a couple IPAs that were hoppy as all get out. Will took to chatting up the cute bartender. As it happened, she had been living in Weed for two years, a long rest after an adolescence of riding the rails. She came to Weed on a whim and decided to stay. Since then she'd been living in a little shanty with a couple friends, and they often took in fellow travelers for a few days. Will considered her for a while but decided against pursuing her any further.

For dinner we met up with Jake's aunt and cousin at a little restaurant in town, then hit the hay. In the morning, Jake worked with his step-grandmother to record a couple of his songs to post on YouTube. It was a simple affair, just Jake on a stool in front of a monotone backdrop. She had nice recording equipment though, so Jake was hopeful the sound would come through clearly. Meanwhile Will and I charted the course for the next leg of our trip. We knew we wanted to hit San Francisco, so we called up what seemed like a promising hotel and booked a room.

We bid the family farewell and made tracks toward San Francisco. We rolled into our freshly booked hotel around 7:00 that evening. In reality it was a quaint little hostel that was only considered a hotel because of the price. We chalked that up to it being Memorial Day weekend. We had to park in a pay lot above a minimart, but the hotel comped that for us.

It was unseasonably cold and the fog had rolled in, but we still set off to find a place to eat. We settled on a little shop called On the Beach Sushi and sat at the bar. The owner was behind the counter prepping our meal for us, so we chatted him up while we ate. Turned out he was from a little town outside of Tokyo. As he put it, he had been in the states for a quarter of a century. He had recently visited Japan and told us that Tokyo was very different, but his town never changed. Jake insisted on ordering Hamachi for everyone on his tab. I hadn't had it at the time but its delicious flavor and Jake's enthusiasm for it has since made it my favorite meat as well.

After a meal of unbelievable sushi and hot sake we headed out. Jake was enlivened. He was hellbent on finding a good club, so we set off on Columbus Street. Within a few blocks we were surrounded by strip clubs. Something had surely gone awry. We stopped the only group that appeared near our age, who happened to be four lesbians, and asked them if there were any good bars around. Their response was simple and to the point:

"You know you're in the strip club district, right?"

We told them that we had surmised as much, but we had happened upon this circumstance through no fault of our own. They suggested that we head back the way we came. We stumbled upon a couple bars, but we were the youngest group by at least a decade in all of them. One was running a special on Tiger beer, which brought back memories for Jake of sitting in a restaurant listening to a group of very inebriated gentlemen enthusiastically shouting for more "TI-GAH!!" Soon that became the rallying cry for our trip.

We continued to aimlessly wander the streets of San Francisco. We would occasionally stop to have a drink at a random bar then move on when it didn't suit our needs. We did find our way into a club at one point, but it just wasn't our scene. We headed back to the hotel to get some rest. By that point, Will was thoroughly in the throes of whatever illness I had brought along, so we bunked together in the double bed assuming I had already built an immunity to it. Jake took the single to avoid contamination.

The next day we spent much of the morning putting around the city. We ended up on a little beach on the edge of town where Will kicked off his shoes and waded a few feet into the water. This was when he made that offhand comment that he had finally stood in every major body of water surrounding the country. I decided I would try to replicate that feat, though as I mentioned before it would be nearly a decade before I would have my chance to set foot in the Atlantic.

For the time being I insisted we stop by City Lights Bookstore as I had read all about it and its founder while studying literature at school. As luck would have it, it was situated very near the strip club district. We had unwittingly wandered right by it the night before. I had hoped to pick up a copy of *On The Road* that had been published by City Lights themselves as a little piece of Beat memorabilia, but failing that I found a copy of *The Original Scroll* and felt satisfied. Will got a postcard and Jake got to set his guitar down for a bit. He had been hoping to gain an audience with some street performing and had therefore been lugging the thing around all day. The store didn't allow any bags though, so Jake jumped at the opportunity to leave it behind the counter.

Afterward we descended into Chinatown to get some food. Jake had roast duck on the brain, so when we found a place with whole birds hanging in the window we felt we'd hit pay dirt. We shared an order of roast duck and wonton soup, and we were glad we'd stopped there. The duck was a bit too fatty for me, but it was delicious nonetheless. Once we had eaten our fill we wandered through the street markets. Jake haggled with the merchants with varying results. I found a number of pipes that Dean and Lucas would have cherished, but they were too pricey to be reasonable, even if I had had the initiative to haggle.

The afternoon was fast getting away from us, so we decided it was time to take off. Our sights were set on the Muir Woods based on a suggestion from Jake's aunt. When we arrived we discovered cars parked as far as a mile away and a visible crowd. We decided we had enough woods in Colorado and took off. We did briefly stop on the precipice above the wood to take in the view. It was lovely, but we pressed on.

We had entertained the notion of taking the 101 down the coast. That would have added hours to the drive and we were pressed as it was, so we took off on I-5 toward Pasadena. I was fascinated with the landscape along the route. Right next to the interstate on the west were massive rolling hills, and to the east were vast plains. Every once in a while we passed a run down farm with a banner proclaiming "Government Created Dust Bowl." The land looked very dry.

Fairly late that night we pulled into Caroline's house, another one of Jake's family friends. She'd apparently gotten bored waiting for us as we could tell she'd tossed back a couple drinks. She was amenable enough though. We spent the night on the floor of her living room and the next day she showed us around town. For dinner we decided to go to the country club she belonged to. Will and I got gussied up and started giving Jake crap that he hadn't brought any clothes nicer than a pair of shorts and a screen printed t-shirt. We thought he would look out of place, but Jake silenced any argument by saying that he never felt compelled to dress up for anyone but himself. We went to dinner and discovered that my version of gussied up was actually the exact outfit all the waitstaff were wearing. It dawned on me that Jake was onto something. I could spend my whole life dressing to impress someone else and still just feel like a damn fool. Better to be comfortable in my own skin.

As nice as Caroline was, we didn't really have all that much in common with her, so we didn't feel compelled to spend much time in her company. We were nearly halfway through the two weeks we had allotted for our trip and we had many more cities to see. From there we cut east and climbed up toward Crestline. Will used to spend his summers working in Disney World and during one season he befriended a guy by the name of Corwin. He lived in a small condo not all that far from Lake Arrowhead, so we decided to pay him a visit while we were in the area. We pulled in late in the afternoon but still managed to arrive before he had gotten off work, so we just sat around outside his door. Corwin was apprenticing as a goldsmith at the time, and he looked every bit the part as he finally came up the walkway. He wore a nice jacket with a very sharp vest underneath. A gold chain ran through one of the buttonholes on his vest and into the pockets on either side. On one end of the chain he kept a fine pocket watch; on the other a pair of spectacles to aid with his more intricate work. He removed all items from the chain to allow him to unbutton the vest and slip into normal clothes for the evening.

There wasn't much we could do since we'd arrived so late, so we entertained ourselves playing Duck Hunt and other games in his house. I fancied myself a decent shot having grown up with an NES. That was until Corwin stood next to the TV, turned so he was facing the opposite end of the condo, and started picking off ducks using a mirror all the way across the room. Will, Jake, and I were clearly outclassed, so we spent the rest of the evening playing Star Fox 64.

The next morning broke on gorgeous weather. We donned our swimsuits and drove over to Lake Arrowhead for some swimming. There was a floating dock a couple dozen yards off shore that the rest of the gang immediately swam to. I was more hesitant. I had never been a good swimmer, and the last time I was in a situation like that I actually exerted myself so hard and in such a panic that I vomited everywhere when I finally got to the dock. I had to be boated back to the shore by a lifeguard shortly thereafter. I wasn't going to be the only one left on the shore this trip though. I swam to the dock, in spite of very similar levels of panic the last few feet, and managed not to puke all over myself this time. We spent an hour or so hanging out on the platform after that. I jumped into the water a few times but never ventured beyond arm's length of the dock.

We did lunch by the shore then Corwin took us bowling. There wasn't all that much to do in Crestline, but we still got a kick out of the idea that the three of us had taken a vacation from the bowling alley in Boulder to go bowl in California. We drank some beer and made an afternoon of it. Then it was time for our last adventure in the area.

Corwin told us that the town had been in somewhat of an uproar because a Hollywood celebrity had bought a humble property in the area. The thing was, it wasn't just him living there. The story went that he had also bought himself a sheep that would wander the yard and bae at all hours of the day. It was just ridiculous enough to be true. We asked Corwin if he knew the address, which of course he did, so we were off to investigate for ourselves. We parked maybe a quarter mile from the property and approached from the back keeping a steady eye in all directions for either the celebrity or the celebrity's sheep. At last we made it nearly to the fence of a normal looking house, but nothing of interest was to be seen. We left a little heartbroken but happy for the diversion.

The next day we headed back west, but this time all the way to Los Angeles. We arrived at the city limits around 8:00 PM and I was galled to discover the highway into town was at a standstill. I could not believe how bad the traffic was. We eventually made it to our destination, which was a house owned by Jake's uncle and his family. This was the last of the progeny of Grandpa James that we had yet to meet. We bedded down there for the night then took a train into the city the next day to explore. We did the normal touristy things, saw the Walk of Fame and whatnot, but ultimately decided this wasn't our scene. The next day we took off for San Diego to meet up with one of Jake's cousins.

Just before we arrived, Jake, Will, and I got into a heated argument about ghosts, death, and the afterlife that left me emotionally charged, so I was actually choking back tears as we met Daren. He was polite enough not to notice and instead offered us some beers. We sat on the patio drinking as he and Jake exchanged stories. One revolved around their Uncle Joe who convinced the whole family to smoke weed at a concert after he himself had just dropped mushrooms. Somehow the best stories of every family revolve around an Uncle Joe.

Daren also told us stories of his roommate Chad who was a notorious drunk around town. He laid out the exact timeline he and a number of former roommates traced as they made this discovery. Upon first moving in, Chad was a gregarious, outgoing guy. He actually seemed like a pretty awesome roommate to have because he knew all the best bars around town, and all the bartenders knew him by name. As the days passed it became apparent that something was amiss as he continually went out, night after night. Eventually everything clicked when Daren went to a bar without him and discovered that all the bartenders knew him because they all *hated* him. From there, only bizarre and upsetting moments ensued.

One day Daren was hanging around the apartment when Chad got home from work. Chad beelined to the fridge, grabbed a beer, and seemed visibly relieved after taking the first few sips. Daren asked if everything was okay, and Chad told him that everything was fine.

"You know those headaches you get when you've gone too long without drinking a beer?" Chad asked. "I just had one of those."

"No," responded Daren, "I don't know those headaches. You're a goddamn alcoholic."

Chad was cordial when we finally did meet him. Surprisingly he chose not to join when we decided to walk to a nearby bar. The four of us had a couple drinks then headed home for the night not long after. The next day we had plans to meet up with Kevin, one of Jake's gaming friends. He ended up taking us sightseeing across town. We had our first taste of In-N-Out Burger with its deceptively simple menu. Kevin surmised that people only really like it for the secret menu. After lunch we bid farewell and hit the road for the last stop on our journey, Las Vegas.

We booked ourselves into the swankiest hotel of the whole journey, again with a single king bed for the three of us to share, then hit the Strip. For the average gawker, a city like Las Vegas really has only one thing to do, one place to go, and that's the Strip. So the city is alive, but in the sense that there is an undulating mass of humans compressed into a single thoroughfare. We entered the torrent of people and did our best not to get swept away. As the light turned green at one intersection a good fifty people flooded the crosswalk. A taxi driver had to physically push his way through the crowd. I was knocked off balance when his bumper tagged my hip. Will and Jake were up ahead and didn't notice.

The hour was late and we were new in town, so we did like we did in Reno and posted up at the slot machines for free drinks. Not much was different between the two cities. In Vegas, the casinos were just a little nicer, the waitresses were just a little prettier, and our money spent just a little faster. We still hardly got drunk, so we decided to descend deeper into the vice of the city. We left the Strip and instead found a little strip club near our hotel. The dancers didn't pay much attention to Jake or myself. Will struck up a conversation with one for a while, but the miles had started catching up to all of us and we soon stumbled back to the hotel.

We had another drink or two while dancing to outrageous music in our room. Jake finally crashed a bit after midnight. I had a heart to heart with Will for an hour or so before he went to bed as well. I joined them shortly thereafter. In spite of being the last to bed I was still the first to rise. The trip had been weighing on all of us heavily, and with just a day and change left I decided to let them sleep. I began watching TV at about 10:00 AM and continued to do so until they roused around 2:00 PM. I've always wondered how sitting in a car for eight hours can be so exhausting. The road has a way of sucking all energy and life right out of me. Fortunately it gives back as much as it takes.

At last we rallied and hit the town. We once again moseyed our way down the Strip, but this time we were deafened by the sound of dozens of men flicking cards featuring the pictures and numbers of escorts. The collective hum reminded me of cicadas in the Midwest. We ducked in and out of the casinos, partly to scope out a good place to gamble and partly to enjoy brief moments of air conditioning. Finally we found a lounge that was about to host a small poker tournament. The buy-in was only thirty dollars so we decided to try our hands. I'd been playing house games at Billy's and thought myself a decent player. I also had a little money I'd saved up from playing pool back home, so I didn't mind throwing down for a bit of gambling. Jake and I were knocked out pretty quick. Will was doing well, but the sight of us milling about with nothing else to do made him lose his appetite for the game so he let himself be knocked out soon after. From there we hit the blackjack table for a while. Jake tried to explain the proper strategies, but my luck was still in the toilet.

After a while we decided it was time to hang up our ill-fated gambling careers. We hit a casino buffet then watched a water show outside the Bellagio. I could hardly believe it up close. Pumps that sounded like cannons firing jets of water sixty feet in the air in the middle of a goddamn desert. I marveled at the audacity of the human species as we sculpt the landscape according to our whims. We called it a night after that.

The next day we set our sights back home. We only had so much time we could spend away from work. M charted the course for us, and we discovered the drive would be about thirteen hours total. Will would take the first four hour shift, I would take the second, and Jake would take whatever was left. The first leg took us out of Nevada via I-15, through the very tip of Arizona, and on to Utah. I'd never been to Arizona before, so I considered telling Will to pull over so I could say I'd stood in the state. This was years before Ray decided to move to Phoenix, so I had no idea that I'd ever be back again, let alone so many times in just a two year period. Regardless, we were already across the border into Utah by the time I made up my mind.

Will made a good clip during his shift, and before I knew it I was taking over. I checked M again and our ETA was exactly nine hours when I started driving. We were just about to get onto I-70 in the heart of Utah, the road that held so many wonders from years past. Something pricked my spirit, and I was off like a flash. Since Will was riding shotgun and in full view of the speedometer I figured he would say something if he disapproved. He didn't say a word about my speed though, so I took free reign to go as fast as I wanted. I would drop to a lagging eighty or eighty-five mph any time I had to navigate a blind corner in case highway patrol was waiting for me, or any time a car came into view ahead and I wasn't sure if they were a cop. When no one was around I pushed the car as hard as I possibly could. I flew down deserted highway stretches with an intensity I had never expressed before nor since. I don't know exactly how fast I went, the speedometer only tracked up to a hundred and ten mph. I do know that by the time my four hour shift was up, M reported that Boulder was just another four hours out. I had shaved a full hour off our drive time. So whatever my top speed was, I had managed to average nearly ninety-four mph for the full drive.

I felt rather accomplished, but we were all too exhausted from two weeks of driving to care. Jake took over and I relaxed for the last leg of our grand adventure. It was rather uneventful, though to our surprise we were hit by a small flurry of snow on the eastern side of the Eisenhower tunnel. We'd gone from a blazing desert to a snowstorm in a matter of hours.

We made it home without any issues in spite of the storm, and so ended the first and only road trip I ever took with Jake. Looking back I'm surprised that I never traveled any more with him. Jake had an unflappable optimism about everything he did. Things didn't always pan out for him, like when he spent that entire day hauling a guitar around the streets of

San Francisco without finding any opportunity to play. His zest for life made the whole journey all the more exciting though. We were hardly in Wyoming before he started exclaiming that he was having the time of his life. He confessed over sushi and sake in San Francisco that he felt the trip was a right of passage for him. His grand outlook on our journey made it all the more meaningful to me as well.

7

In August of 2008 Will was heading down to Florida to fulfill
a commitment at Disney World. He'd been working for the
park as a seasonal employee for a few years, and to maintain
his status he had to spend at least three days there before the
end of the month. His unflinching sense of duty kept him
from blowing off the commitment altogether even though he
was loathe to make the thirty hour drive from his new home
in Boulder. As a result, he was looking for friends to ride with
him and share in his Disney Experience when he wasn't on
duty. By that time I'd accepted that my grand motorcycle trip
had fallen to pieces, so I had a few thousands bucks in my
bank account with nothing in particular to spend it on. We got
our shifts covered at the bowling alley and set off.

On our first day we crossed the southern lands of Colorado,
the panhandle of Oklahoma, and the vast expanse of Texas.

Our destination that day was Austin, Texas where Will's friend Christi had offered to put us up for the night. Christi also did seasonal work at Disney, so Will had coordinated with her to head down that same week. We pulled into her apartment in time to share a few drinks with her and her friends before we crashed on the floor.

The next morning we set off as a loose convoy toward New Orleans to get the last member of our crew. Christi was taking her own car so she could leave later in the morning and have a little more freedom around her trip. As we were crossing a bridge near Baton Rouge we suddenly went from clear sunny skies to the most wicked downpour I'd seen in my life. If such a storm hit Colorado people would be huddled inside thinking it was the end of days. I was driving at the time and thought about slowing to a crawl, but then I looked over and saw Will paying no mind to the weather. It occurred to me that this was par for the course down in the Gulf, so if I slowed down I very well might be rear ended by a local who'd driven this weather every day of his life. I kept chugging at an even fifty-five until it passed, praying all the while that there wasn't another tourist ahead of me that would suddenly slam on the brakes like I had considered.

The storm passed as quickly as it came and soon we arrived in New Orleans, the home of Will's long time friend Kelly. At the time she was living in a one bedroom apartment with her friend Alan. They were both gay and had no interest in each other whatsoever, but they had sold themselves as a hetero couple to convince the property owners to rent them the cheaper single unit. The real arrangement was that Kelly slept in the bedroom and Alan was full time in the living room. It didn't seem to bother him much, and we spent the afternoon watching Olympic Gymnastics on his couch / bed while trying to guide Christi to the apartment complex over the phone. This was when we first realized her sense of direction was severely impaired. She finally made it though, and we gave no more thought to the matter.

Since this was my first time in New Orleans we had to hit Bourbon Street. It wasn't quite time to start partying though, so we first ran to a grocery store to stock up for the trip ahead. Will and Kelly tried to tell me stories about the laissez-faire alcohol laws in the area as we were shopping. They claimed that everyone in the car, driver included, could be actively drinking as long as the one at the wheel was still under the legal limit. I couldn't even process the idea because I was staring dumbly at racks of liquor in the grocery store. In my twenty years of life I had never seen such a thing. Keep in mind, Colorado had just legalized the sale of alcohol on Sundays a few weeks before our trip, and that had been enough to blow my mind.

Soon it was time to make our way to the land of debauchery. We parked our car somewhere in the French Quarter, waited for Christi to catch up, and hit the town. I nearly stopped dead in my tracks when I saw the first drunk person stumble out of a bar, drink still in hand, and wander by a mounted cop. That was legal here? Drinking on the street itself? Not only that, there were also drink vendors who *only operated streetside?*

Will made a beeline toward one such stand and came back with a neon green plastic tube that was roughly a foot tall with a base shaped like a hand grenade. Will explained to me that the aptly named Hand Grenade was a right of passage for tourists passing through New Orleans. We took a quick turn down a side street and emerged back on Bourbon a moment later with the drink in my hand and no one the wiser. I then had a chance to examine it up close. The contents were as green as the glass itself. I took a sip and discovered it tasted like citrusy syrup with no trace of alcohol whatsoever, yet it had the strange effect of making me walk and talk funny. It was a double shot of headaches and bad decisions. I couldn't stop drinking it.

I had just finished the Hand Grenade when we arrived at our final destination. I was about to throw the cup away on the street when Will told me to carry it in. The bartender glanced at my empty drink and asked what I would have for the next round. Age limits and IDs never entered the conversation. The mainstay brew of New Orleans was Abita, so I ordered one of those in what would become a longstanding tradition of mine of purposely seeking out the local beers of any place I traveled. It was pale and refreshing, exactly what I wanted on a hot summer night as the humidity crossed into ungodly territory. I was also just happy for something to water down the fiery contents of my belly.

As our group settled in for some old fashioned catching up as only alcohol could facilitate, I started glancing around the inside of the bar. Above us, exposed cross beams ran the full width of the building. I noticed some odd decorations, and it took my alcohol-addled brain a minute to realize that every joist was crowded with badges from retired police officers. That's when a comment that had slipped my mind came roaring back with full force. Will and Kelly had decided that the first bar to serve me a drink, just five months after my twentieth birthday, should be a bar owned by a couple of retired New Orleans cops.

We had a few more drinks there as the night progressed. Eventually I had to hit the head, as one often does in those situations, and I was surprised to see that there were no locks on the door of the one-toilet bathroom. I asked Kelly about it when I got back to the party and she responded, "Yeah, they don't want any heroin addicts to lock themselves in and pass out." That line of reasoning made perfect sense at the time, which was when I knew I'd had too much to drink. We paid our tab and headed back to Kelly's apartment. Will, Christi, and I passed out on the floor of the single bedroom so that Alan would have some privacy in the living room. In the morning, Will was kind enough to take the first driving shift as I was still reeling from the night before.

With that we finally set off for Orlando. We made a quick pit stop early in the day at Gulfport, Mississippi to see Will's dad. He did the fatherly thing and sent us along with a few bottles of wine in case we ran out. We waved our goodbyes and hit the road across the itty bits of Mississippi and Alabama, then the unbearably long panhandle of Florida.

Will navigated us to what would be our humble abode for the next few days. We were on Disney property but in one of the more modest accommodations. They had amassed a number of trailers, styled them to look like log cabins, and manicured the surroundings to resemble a campground all the way down to the communal charcoal grills.

Will and Christi would be starting work in the morning, so we decided to have another night of drinking. Christi had gotten separated from us on the trip though and hadn't arrived at the trailer yet. We didn't want to start the party without her, so we turned on the Olympics, Marksmanship this time, and set about waiting. An hour passed with no word from her. By that time we were watching the news as the weatherman carefully traced the formation and expected path of Tropical Storm Fay. It was still days away from hitting Florida, so I paid it little mind. Instead I excused myself to the bedroom, of which there was one in the entire trailer, and gave Crystal a call to regale her with our adventures so far.

We had just begun dating a couple weeks earlier, so I wanted to build up some emotional capital and offset the fact that I was on my second cross-country road trip without her since we met. We talked for an hour or so then closed with Crystal cautioning me to be careful and not drink too much. I came back to the living room to discover Will was just getting off the phone with Christi, who was still lost. I started laughing hysterically. Will gave me a troubled look, but Kelly knew how I felt. She exclaimed, "You have to laugh to keep from crying," and joined in. Will cracked a smile, but he was still too upset to see the humor in it.

Another hour passed before Christi arrived, and we were just about to break into a big bottle of Bacardi when Crystal's words echoed through my head. Be careful, don't drink too much. We were still in that strange phase where we were shaping ourselves to be the person we thought the other wanted us to be. So I suddenly announced, "I'm not going to drink." Will had reached his breaking point about two hours earlier, so he turned to me exasperated and asked what the hell I was on about. I stupidly decided to dig my heels in and refused to partake. A short argument ensued and we all went to bed with a dark cloud over our heads. So ended our first day in the happiest goddamn place on Earth.

Will and Christi were off to work bright and early the next morning, which was when the reality of the situation finally dawned on me. Since those two were there for a job I would hardly see them, so the vast majority of my time would be spent alone with Kelly. She was a Disney veteran though and didn't seem too put off by my introverted tendencies, so we wandered from ride to ride, making the most of the free three-day passes that Will had scored for us. The day progressed with little of note, but that evening was something to behold. There was an after-hours event, a chance for parents to spend more money on top of the exorbitant admission fee for an extra two hours of rides after the riffraff had been ushered out. We had access as part of the whole package, so as soon as our comrades ended their shift we hurried to our trailer, downed a few shots, and headed back to the park. Needless to say, I was on much better terms with both Will and alcohol that evening

We made it back in time to catch the fireworks show. In most parts of the country a display that size would be the Fourth Of July Jubilee. At Disney it was a typical Friday. Will told me they budgeted ten thousand dollars per day for fireworks alone. Fuck me. Afterward we roared around the park in a drunken stupor, clamoring on rides and sidestepping parents that were desperately trying to create a magical family vacation before they strangled their kids.

The next few days were mostly more of the same. Wandering the parks by day, drinking together by night. Just before the trip began I had learned that Crystal collected shot glasses, so a decent amount of my time was occupied trying to find some good ones for her. One night I held up our escapades for nearly an hour as I scoured every gift shop I could find, agonizing over which design she would like best. Ultimately I bought two stemmed ones with a whole tulip affair going on up top.

Will was always eager to give us the behind-the-scenes scoop on Disney. As he told it, the highest paid park staff were the actors in the full body costumes as that amounted to a Disney version of hazard pay. According to Will, they would spend fifteen minutes of every hour outside taking photos with their adoring fans and blindly signing autographs. Blindly was an apt description as the actor's viewing hole rarely lined up with the eyes of the costume. Each actor was grilled relentlessly before their first public appearance to ensure they could perfectly recreate the appropriate signature without looking. No parent wanted to explain to their kids why Eeyore was holding their autograph book up to his neck when he went to sign it. But I digress. The other forty-five minutes of each hour was spent in an air conditioned room, encased in ice packs, panting like a dog.

After three days in the park Will's commitment was fulfilled and it was time to set off for New Orleans. We considered staying longer, but Tropical Storm Fay was knocking at Florida's doorstep. We got out about a day ahead of it, which was fortunate for us as its erratic path caused the storm to make landfall a record four times across Florida. It traced much of the path we would take out of the state, and weather data indicated it spun off fifty tornadoes across five states before petering out somewhere over Kentucky.

Before we left the park, Will took us to the "backstage" store so I could continue my crusade for the perfect shot glass. This was the employee-only shop that contained out of season and discontinued merchandise, so it promised to be the one place I could find a rare collectible. I might have had more luck if I was looking for a more common item, but shot glasses were in short supply. I found one from St. Patrick's Day featuring Mickey in green shorts with matching shoes, vest, and bowler hat. I bought it more for the story than anything else.

Our drive through Florida was wet but mostly unremarkable. We dropped Kelly off at her apartment in the mid-afternoon then charted a course to Boulder. We had left Christi in our dust at Disney, so we were under no obligation to detour through Austin. Will and I decided that we didn't want to stop at a hotel anywhere along the route, so I would take most of the daylight driving and leave the graveyard shift to him. I got mixed up going around Dallas-Fort Worth and wasted a half hour as I inadvertently circled the metroplex and headed back east a ways. After we sorted that out we soon found ourselves in the open air of Northern Texas. I didn't expect the land to be so beautiful in those parts. At face value it was a great desolate expanse, but I found a sort of peace out there that I haven't seen in much of the country.

As darkness set in we stopped at a little gas station to switch places. Will took the wheel and popped an Adderall so he'd have the focus to make it through the night. The last thing I remember before I drifted off to sleep was us barreling down the highway at sixty-five when a pack of jackrabbits appeared out of nowhere. We went from wide open road as far as the headlights could shine to a minefield of animals in a matter of moments. Will navigated as best he could, but just as we'd nearly cleared the colony he caught one with both wheels on the driver's side. I stifled the gasp in my throat, steadied my voice, and said, "There was nothing you could do."

About nine hours later I awoke to the sun rising in Colorado as we were approaching Castle Rock. I looked over to see a wide-eyed Will with a death grip on the wheel. Despite his grave expression, his voice hardly wavered as he told me, "You *have* to drive now." We pulled off at a rest stop so I could splash some water on my face and take the wheel. Will tried his best to shut his eyes, but he was still jittery from the Adderall. I got us home as quick as I could so we could both spend the rest of our day crashed in bed.

After my trip through California with Will and Jake, and my trip to the East Coast with Crystal, I was feeling the pull back to the Gulf. It was a ritual by then. I would visit the East Coast one year, the Gulf Coast the next year, the West Coast after that, then repeat the process. Crystal and I were celebrating our third year together, and I convinced her and Will to accompany me down to New Orleans. This time we started our journey heading due west through Kansas before turning south through Oklahoma, Texas, and northern Louisiana. Emboldened by the fact that we had an additional member in our party we once again decided to make the drive in a single day. Crystal and I took the brunt of the driving while it was light out. As darkness settled in I stretched out in the backseat and Crystal reclined in the front while Will ushered us through the night.

He woke us at dawn near Shreveport, Louisiana, to let us know that we were being pulled over. At that point I decided I should never sleep in the backseat of cars as I was starting to see a theme. The officer wrote Will a hundred and fifty dollar ticket for going seven over the speed limit on the interstate. More than likely it was actually for going seven over the speed limit with Colorado plates. There was no doubt in

Will's mind that we'd been singled out since we wouldn't be around to fight the ticket in court. As soon as Will's driving shift was over he began researching remote representation. He figured paying a lawyer seventy-five bucks to get the ticket dismissed would placate his indignant rage. He never managed to make such arrangements.

We crossed the rest of Louisiana without incident and made our way onward to Mississippi. Will wanted to swing by Gulfport to say hi to his dad Stockton since we were in the area, so Crystal and I decided to postpone our New Orleans adventure for an hour. That quickly became a few hours as we were invited to stay for dinner.

More accurately, we were hanging out and then we absolutely had to leave right away for one of the nearby casinos. We got there, Stockton paid, then he sat down and waited. I saw a full buffet laid out before me so I piled up a plate and came back to the table. That's when Stockton gave me a disappointed look. Apparently the idea was to get there just minutes before the price was set to jump from the lunch rate to the more expensive dinner rate. So he got us in for cheap and expected us to wait the twenty minutes until they brought out the king crab legs. Oh well. I didn't need crab that day anyway.

The hour had gotten late when we finally returned home. We decided to spend the night there and delay our New Orleans trip until morning. Stockton had a pull out in his office that was just big enough for Crystal and I to share, and Will spent the night on the couch in the living room. The next morning I was eager to set off for Louisiana, but Will suggested we stay another day in Gulfport. Stockton had offered to buy a few pounds of boiled crawfish for dinner to give us an authentic

Gulf Coast experience. I finally realized that my big trip to New Orleans was actually Will's big trip to visit his dad. I was a little annoyed, but I couldn't blame him. It wasn't like I had any grand vision for the trip. My plan amounted to going to New Orleans and getting really drunk. I hadn't even booked a hotel ahead of time, so I didn't argue as we shifted focus to a family vacation. I had to admit I was eager to try real cajun crawfish anyway.

Stockton lived about a mile down the shore from the grocery store, so we walked along the beach to pick up supplies. I was eager to get my feet wet in the Gulf. It had been two years since Will gave me the idea of setting foot in every body of water that surrounded the country, and I still had yet to step in either the Gulf or the Atlantic. My excitement quickly faded when I discovered there had been a jellyfish bloom that week, and damn near every square foot of sand had a translucent carcass on it. Will and his dad assured me that they were not a stinging kind, so I made sure to get both feet in the water before hanging way up on the shore. Dangerous or not they were disgusting to step on.

A mile there, a mile back, and we were set to make dinner. We came home with a giant bag of crawfish and all the fixins. Stockton prepared the meal while I mulled over a serious matter. I had heard that some people suck the juice from the crawfish heads after finishing the tail meat. I'd been thinking about this idea all day and had come to the conclusion that I would suck the head just to see what it was like. However, just as we were sitting down to dinner, Stockton made a comment that *some* people suck the heads, clearly intimating that he didn't think highly of anyone who would conduct themselves in such a manner. He had some particular ideas about decorum and I did not want to run afoul of them. To be fair, Will's dad was an empirically good man. He worked as a trauma doctor in a local E.R. most of the year, and in his off months he would travel to Africa to work as a doctor in impoverished areas. Who was I to come into his home and offend him by sucking the head of a crawfish?

There was an art to getting the tail meat out which came with practice. It took about an hour and a half, but I finally ate enough crawfish, one morsel at a time, to really feel satisfied. Crystal was a trooper and ate dinner without complaint even though she hated, as she described it, "dissecting her own food." After dinner we sat down in the living room to play a board game of Stockton's own design. He had first created it when he was a kid, and he'd been revising it in the intervening decades. The gist was that each player was assigned a list of errands at the beginning then they competed to see who could finish theirs first as they navigated a miniature city. If nothing else it was a relaxing way to spend the evening, which would sharply juxtapose our activities the following night.

The next morning the four of us, Will's dad included, drove across state lines to New Orleans. It had been a while since Stockton had been there and he wanted to see it again. We ate lunch together and wandered the French Quarter a bit. He was kind enough to book us a room in a very posh hotel near Bourbon Street. It was rather unexpected, but recall that he was an empirically good guy. Shortly thereafter Stockton politely excused himself to head back home and leave us to our own debaucherous plans. Kelly came to join us, except by then she had transitioned to a man and was calling himself Fletcher. I insisted that we begin with Hand Grenades for Crystal and myself. Neither Fletcher nor Will could believe I was so excited to relive that experience. They explained to Crystal that locals could always tell when tourists were in the area because of the iridescent green puke in the gutters just off Bourbon Street. Undeterred, Crystal joined me for one.

We spent some time wandering Bourbon Street proper until we got bored, at which point Fletcher suggested we check out one of his favorite strip clubs. Crystal didn't seem to mind so we ventured onward. I should say that Crystal didn't mind until we got in there and all the strippers had smaller breasts than she did. We paid to see a show after all. Fletcher would periodically disappear and show up again with another round of shots that we happily tossed back. We were there for an hour, maybe two, before the Hand Grenades started catching up with us. Crystal and I made our way back to the hotel where Crystal promptly got sick for the next hour or so. Once she had thoroughly emptied her stomach we decided to hit the hay. Will and Fletcher rolled in a couple hours later, also ready to sleep. I didn't ask them what they'd gotten up to after we parted ways.

Crystal soldiered on the next morning despite a wicked hangover. We walked about the city a little more, saw the mighty Mississippi River, and finally made our way to Café Du Monde for breakfast beignets. We skipped the wait as we accidentally walked in a back way and sat down at an empty table. Beignets at Café Du Monde was a New Orleans staple that I had missed on my last trip, and it was inarguably a better tradition than Hand Grenades on Bourbon Street. The beignets were fried pillows of dough piled so high with powdered sugar that when I made the mistake of breathing within twelve inches of one I nearly asphyxiated. When I finally bit into one I discovered the insides were so perfectly fluffy that for a moment I feared I actually did die a powdered sugar related death and was taking my first heavenly meal in the great beyond.

Not long afterward we bid farewell to Fletcher and headed east for one more night with Stockton. At that point Will was getting pretty wishy-washy, suggesting that he might stay in Mississippi for a while rather than drive back with us. He could catch a plane when he finally did want to get back to Colorado. Of course, that plane could just as likely be pointed to the Carolinas to see the rest of his family instead. We were not surprised when morning came and he told us to hit the road without him.

Seeing as we were down a driver, Crystal and I had no intention of making the return trip in a single day. We booked a room in Oklahoma City for the night, which meant we had some extra time to explore the region. During my previous trip down south I had only gotten Crystal shot glasses from Florida, so she was eager so fill her collection with items from all the neighboring states. After a quick jaunt west to Louisiana we cut a path up north to Arkansas. We crossed the border into Texas at the great city of Texarkana. The whole idea of having a city that spans two states seemed bizarre to me. Being from Colorado, the closest thing I saw was the city of Kanorado, Kansas. That's a good ten miles east of the Colorado border though, so not a true two state town at all. Colorado has no interest in that shit I suppose.

We swung north from Texas on our final stretch toward Oklahoma City. We were about an hour outside the city when we were hit by one of the most incredible thunderstorms I've seen in my life. It was well past sunset and great forks of lightning lit up the sky at regular intervals. We were so blown away I called my dad to find out if there were any tornado warnings in the area. He told me the reports were all saying severe thunderstorms, no tornados, so we pressed on. We got to town, checked in, and discovered we'd been assigned a room on the ground floor. We looked around the area to see if we were in a flood zone. It didn't seem like it, but we kept our suitcase off the ground just in case.

We still needed dinner though. We thought about grabbing something from the vending machine, but a Google search of the area revealed there was a Steak 'n Shake a couple miles away. Having no idea when we would be able to patronize our beloved fast food chain again we bundled up and hit the road. After crossing multiple pools of standing water a foot or more deep and enduring a blowing rain so strong we couldn't see out one side of the car we arrived at the drive through. We placed our order and when the cashier handed us the food she seemed legitimately terrified that we had braved the weather to darken her door. We probably were crazy for doing it, but she had to have been just as crazy for keeping the grill going during that storm. Fortunately, the weather had cleared up by the following morning, and we made our way back home without event.

A couple weeks later Will finally returned to Colorado. He had detoured through North Carolina after all. He felt bad for leaving us to find our own way home and even offered to pay for our gas. I shrugged off his generosity. As I said, I didn't begrudge him for anything in Mississippi. Those two trips I took with him down south may have been the only times he'd gotten back to see his family in three years, and that must have been hard on him. He hadn't left the Gulf by choice.

He'd been in school in Louisiana when Katrina hit. Afterward it just wasn't possible for him to continue until his college had time to rebuild. The University of Colorado was one school accepting transfers from students impacted by the disaster, so Will decided to follow his little sister out west. That's how the two of us came to meet. He did a lot to expand my worldview over the few years we worked and traveled together, so there was no need for him to offer me anything more.

8

In the summer of 2014 I found myself in a car with my aunt and my cousin as we retraced the old route from Colorado to my grandparents' house in Madison, Wisconsin. When I was a child, few things in the world brought me more joy than seeing my grandparents. Back in the days when I had more fingers on my hands than years to my name they would make the trek out to see us in Colorado. As all of us got older and it became easier for our family to make the journey than for them, we made it a yearly tradition to visit them each summer. The first few years we went via plane, but when that got too expensive we decided to drive the whole way.

So each summer we made the familiar trip up along highway 52 until we reached I-76. We would follow that through the remainder of Colorado, past the teepee rest stop just on the very boundary of our state. From there I-80 would take us all the way through Nebraska and most of the way through Iowa. Just about Cedar Rapids we would take smaller highways up through the remainder of Iowa, across the mighty Mississippi, and into Madison. The entire endeavor took about seventeen hours with stops, of which there were many.

I must have made that trip more than a dozen times in my life, and each time we added to the lore of our travels. One year we saw a ten ton truck full of potatoes turned over in the streets of Fort Lupton. Another year had spider encounters at some of the more unsavory rest stops in Wisconsin. Those vacations were the first experience I ever had with real road trips. I would say that the excitement of new adventures each summer combined with the unbridled joy of seeing my family was probably what engendered my love of the road.

The circumstances surrounding our 2014 trip were not so elevating. After years battling Alzheimer's my grandfather had passed away the month before. We left on a Thursday to mourn with the family in Madison. We planned to spend Friday, Saturday, and Sunday with everyone, then return to Colorado on Monday. The memorial service for my grandpa would be held on Saturday.

The trip itself was relatively uneventful. We had a little scare while I was at the wheel outside of Des Moines. Traffic came to a stop before I realized it, but only the tires and brakes were worse for the wear as I came to a screeching halt just in time. My cousin took over the driving responsibility after that and we made decent time to Madison. When we finally got there we met up with the rest of the family for dinner. We came to the realization that this was the first time all four grandkids of the family were together at once. It's strange how death has a way of bringing the family together. A photo exists somewhere of all of us sitting on a couch trying to look happy in spite of the circumstances. Families make the most of the opportunities presented to them I suppose. As the night wore on my aunt, my cousin, and I retired to the hotel room we were sharing across town.

At about 9:00 AM on Saturday morning, as I was pressing the shirt I would wear to my grandpa's memorial a few hours later, we heard the screaming. My aunt couldn't quite make out the words, but I heard it clearly, "Someone shot my boyfriend." A woman was screaming that as she ran through the hotel hallway. I thought it was a really bad joke until a few seconds later she came back down the hall still wailing for someone to help her.

What shocked me most about the situation was how quickly my aunt reacted. Without a pause she jumped up and began chasing down the woman to find out what happened. That's one quality that did not fall on my branch of the family tree. I've never known what to do in emergencies. Whether my aunt knew what to do or not, she immediately began to manage the situation. She told us to call 9-1-1 while she tried to get ahold of the screaming woman. Since my cousin had his phone closer at hand he began dialing as he followed the others outside. I, on the other hand, took my time trailing after them. I had a sense of what I was going to see when I stepped out to the parking lot. There was no way to avoid it, but I wanted to postpone it as long as possible. I took a moment to make sure the room was in order. I switched off the television, unplugged the iron, steeled myself for the scene to come, and walked outside.

My cousin was on the phone giving the dispatcher directions while my aunt stood ready to wave down the ambulance. Maybe ten yards away the frantic woman stood over a man who was lying face down on the concrete. He was completely motionless with a large stream of blood coiling away from his body. I stood awkwardly by the doorway, not really knowing what to do or where to look. Was it taboo to stare at a dead man in the street? Either way, I felt it would be inappropriate for me to walk away from the situation before it concluded. That wouldn't be long though as the paramedics soon arrived. They must have realized the guy was dead as they pulled up because they didn't appear to be in any rush to get to him. As a show of good faith they brought a defibrillator, but they never used it. They simply knelt beside him, felt for a pulse, and pronounced him dead.

The wail that came out of the frantic woman was unlike anything I had ever heard before or since in my life. It was the sound of unbridled anguish as her life crumbled in front of her eyes. She collapsed onto the pavement and screamed for what seemed like a very long time. She scraped her knees on the concrete and I remember thinking that must have really stung. I doubt she noticed though.

My family and I mostly hid in our room for the next hour. We would have left altogether had our car not been cordoned off by police tape. The few times I did venture into the hallways I saw a myriad of different emotions wash over the bereaved woman. She fluctuated from lucidly describing the shooting for the police to sobbing uncontrollably. Once when I walked by she was sitting in a chair, looking at nothing in particular, absently saying, "I've never seen a dead body before."

That's the thing with death: it not only affects different people in different ways, it affects *the same person* in different ways. Sometimes in very outlandish ways. Case in point, one of my most bizarre brushes with death came during the semester I spent living with Flynn, Sterling, and Miles in a house we affectionately dubbed The Murder House.

As young men in the rental market we had to accept that a certain number of foul deeds had occurred in any property we looked at. So when the four of us were desperately trying to find a place in the January off-season and a house came on the market at a ridiculously low price, we didn't ask questions. At a mere eighteen hundred dollars per month for a six-bedroom house with a fenced yard we were willing to turn a blind eye to just about anything. While touring the place we eagerly discussed where we'd put the ping pong table, the Xbox, and the music equipment.

It wasn't until we were actually moving in that we noticed the evidence stickers on every entrance of the house. That was weird, but we figured it was probably something left from an out of hand party long before. Then we discovered evidence bags in our cupboards. That's when it really hit home that a serious crime had been committed in the house very recently. We did some digging and found our address mentioned in an article from the prior August. Evidently the previous renter was stabbed to death in our kitchen four months before we moved in. His wife had driven a kitchen knife nine inches into his chest, though she was later acquitted when it was found to be in self-defense.

As I said before, renters have to accept that certain things have undoubtedly happened in the past, but those things are usually impossible to know and therefore easy to ignore. We didn't have that luxury anymore once we learned that the last tenant spent his final moments bleeding out on the floor in our kitchen. The next two days were spent generally freaking out. We bitched amongst ourselves about what we would have done had we known, and we consulted lawyers to find out if it was legal for the landlord to withhold that sort of information. It turned out that yes, it was completely legal. A landlord in Boulder was only required to disclose issues that may pose physical harm to the tenants. There was no such requirement for information that would only cause emotional harm.

So after those first few days had passed, and it was clear that we weren't going to do anything about the situation, we made our peace with it. That's when we began referring to our place as The Murder House. In truth, we got a little too comfortable with it when Liam looked up the image of the deceased and printed a cardboard cut out of him to haunt us. We made a game of hiding him around the house. I would pull back the covers on my bed and discover him lying in wait for me. Then I would position him on the toilet so Flynn would find him when he went for his morning constitutional.

The average person would probably think this was abhorrent behavior, and I wouldn't blame them. All I can say is that we did whatever would keep us sane. Being constantly reminded of the inevitability of death could have driven all of us out of our minds. We had to decide not to let it get to us. It probably helped that we had never met the guy in our lives. I could say to myself that sometimes people just die, as they have since the world began, and go about my day. When it came to the death of one of my own friends, I didn't take it in such a lighthearted stride.

Years before that I had lost a friend when he drowned in a lake outside Boulder. He and a group of guys were swimming at night. I wasn't there, so I can only describe what I've heard after the fact. The story was that they were swimming to a pier, when out of nowhere Jonah started complaining that something was wrong. Before anyone could do anything he went under. Rescue divers pulled his body out a few hours later. There was a standing-room-only funeral service for him a couple weeks later. It felt like all of Boulder turned out to mourn his death. All of us had been touched by his life and untimely death. For my own part, I cried at the funeral then pushed it out of my head. Of course, something like that has a way of pushing itself back in at unexpected times.

Late in the summer of 2012 a group of us were down in Roswell, New Mexico, due to a geographic oddity. Liam was stationed in San Angelo, Texas, and he had to stay within a five hour radius of base at all times unless he requested leave. Ray was still out in Phoenix, and the rest of us were living in Boulder. So what city was within Liam's limits, and roughly equidistant between Boulder and Phoenix? It turned out Roswell was.

The drive itself wasn't too bad. There was one hairy moment coming over Raton pass when, in spite of rather nice weather all round, we hit a wet spot at eighty mph and hydroplaned just long enough to begin redirecting the nose of the car. In that moment we were aware that things could turn *really* bad and we were just waiting to see if it did or not. If we had gone another few seconds Nick would have needed to make some frantic correction to keep from sliding sideways down the highway on a five percent grade.

The road cleared up in time to give us a stomach-turning lurch when the wheels hit dry pavement but nothing more. It warranted a passing comment, but I'm not sure we mentioned it to Ray or Liam when we finally met up with them. Nick, Jed, and I were the first to arrive, so we scouted the local Applebee's looking for a rendezvous point where we could grab some dinner. When the other two showed up, we had forgotten anything that happened on our journey as the elation of being with each other washed over us. We caught up while we ate dinner, then hit a local liquor store for libations. Our shopping list included the usual assortment of half-decent booze, but just as we were about to check out something caught my eye. On a whim I bought a bottle of tequila shaped like a six-shooter. It seemed befitting of our time in the desert. We took everything back to the single hotel room we had booked for the five of us and made a night of it.

The next day we visited the International UFO Museum & Research Center. It was anyone's guess what sort of research they conducted. Our walk through the museum only ate up an hour or two of our trip, so we had to find other excursions. Thus we decided to visit the Bottomless Lakes State Park about fifteen miles outside of town. The park had eleven lakes in total with the largest being a favorite hangout spot of the area. There was plenty of water for swimming, and the five of us rented a paddle boat and a couple paddleboards. At least, the staff called them paddleboards. Really they were nothing more than an elongated piece of styrofoam, utterly impossible for anyone to stand on. Each of us tried and failed miserably.

The only stipulation for renting the equipment was to wear life vests while we were over the ninety-foot deep end of the lake. We all made a good show of wearing them at first, but eventually Nick got tired of his vest, tossed it aside, and dove in. I don't know if it was our close call on Raton pass or the sudden memory of Jonah drowning in a similar lake, but I freaked out on Nick. He hardly batted an eye as I was yelling at him to put his vest back on. He was a strong swimmer, he had actually lived on a houseboat for years, so a quick dip in the lake was nothing to him.

I can say now that I was definitely making too much of the situation, but there's just no telling how or when death will affect any of us. We may cry, we may laugh, we may go ballistic. Hell, we may do all three at once. There's really no means to prepare ourselves for it. Reminding ourselves that sometimes people just die gets a lot scarier when we realize those people could be us. We try to rationalize that thought away. Of the stories I've told so far, one might say, "Sure, sometimes arguments get out of hand, and people do scary stuff, but if I keep a level head I can avoid being stabbed in my own kitchen. And yeah, some activities are inherently dangerous, and all the more when they are done without professional supervision of, say, a lifeguard. But if I avoid risky situations I'll be fine." I can understand that thinking, but the fact remains that sometimes people just die, no matter the circumstance.

My mother-in-law was walking on a treadmill at her gym, something she did all the time. The staff there saw her and didn't notice anything wrong. At some point, she stopped the machine, stepped off, and collapsed. Two paramedics were working out right next to her and immediately began CPR while the staff called 9-1-1. They continued to work on her all the way to the emergency room. They never got a pulse.

My mother-in-law was not doing anything risky. She had professionals right there to help if something went wrong. She had every conceivable chance to live, but she didn't.

Sometimes people just die.

9

Having visited the East Coast and Gulf Coast together, Crystal and I decided to complete our circuit of America in 2012 with a journey through the Pacific Northwest. On my previous trip through California with Jake and Will, I brought my journal along to jot down our experiences while they were fresh in my mind. I'm pretty glad I didn't do the same during my tour with Crystal. That would have put me too close to the events of the trip as they were happening. No, this was the sort of endeavor I had to take a step back from and assess with a clear head before passing judgement upon it.

We set off from Boulder in high spirits. We were driving my Mazda 626 at the time. The Icebox was long gone and our previous road trips had all been in Crystal's RAV4, so I figured it was time to put some miles on my new vehicle. We engaged in minor chit chat and had a few laughs. Somewhere near the Wyoming border I asked Crystal what a group of gorillas was called because that was relevant for some reason. She couldn't remember, so she pulled up a website on her phone to find out. I had to take a moment and marvel at how quickly technology had advanced. Two years before I had to *pay* for a navigation app that was so terrible it told us to pull off the road at every exit. This trip Crystal was discovering that a group of gorillas was called a band, a gathering of buffalo was an obstinacy, and there was no name for a group of koalas all while we cruised through northern Colorado.

That entertained us until we merged onto I-80 near Laramie. From there we were occupied by the unyielding onslaught of Little America billboards. We learned that it was a hotel chain across the West, though the real Little America was located at Exit 68, Little America, WY 82929 because it was literally a city unto itself. While they were a pleasant diversion, the ads were no doubt the bane of many a family vacation. They appear every ten miles or so, and the most prominent amenity advertised was the fifty cent ice cream cone, enticing children to insist their parents pull off. For those that successfully resisted the siren song of Little America, one final billboard just past town cheerfully advised that another Little America could be found in only a few hundred miles.

We may have enjoyed one of those ice cream cones ourselves if my car had broken down a little sooner. As it was, we were maybe thirty miles past Little America when the engine temp started redlining. Crystal was driving at the time and was boxed in by three semis, which didn't make pulling over very easy. She accelerated around one of them and got off near a small exit. We popped the hood and discovered my overflow coolant reservoir had a crack across the top. We waited around for twenty minutes until the engine was cool enough for me to work the cap off with a stick. I was spared from an eruption of coolant, possibly because the reservoir itself was bone dry. It took a little more than a quart of water to fill it back up.

If I had any sense in my head I would have said we should turn back. We would lose a day of travel, but we could have set off again in the morning using Crystal's car and wouldn't be much worse off. We were on a timetable though. Sakka wanted to be part of the trip, but she couldn't join us for the first leg of the drive due to another engagement. Instead, she had booked a flight to Eugene, Oregon, where we would meet up with her, then the three of us would continue on to Seattle, Spokane, and home. We convinced ourselves that whatever the problem was we could diagnose and fix it in Ogden that night then continue on as scheduled.

We pulled into Uncle Seb's house later that evening amid a cloud of steam billowing from the crack in the reservoir. We put the car out of our minds for a bit as we were greeted by a large contingent of Crystal's family. Of course there was her aunt and uncle and cousins from Ogden. Her family from Kemmerer, Wyoming, had also come out to see us for the evening. The decision was made to grab dinner at a nearby BYOB sushi place, the concept of which thoroughly baffled Crystal and myself. Walking into a restaurant with multiple six-packs of beer seemed outrageous to us. The proprietors didn't say anything about it though, so we quickly cozied up to the idea.

Dinner was spent mostly reminiscing about all the times their family had blacked out drinking and done crazy shit together.

Usually that occurred on cruise ships, but their antics were by no means limited to the high seas. I thoroughly enjoyed my meal. I always loved that side of Crystal's family, and not just because they were hilarious and crass and crazy. I loved them because they were the most authentic people I've met in my life. It didn't matter where they were or what they were doing, they were always just exactly who they were.

After dinner Uncle Seb drove me over to a local shop that had a new overflow reservoir for my car. We swapped it in and I was sure that was the end of our troubles. The next day we said our goodbyes and continued west. Soon Crystal would experience the Bonneville Salt Flats for the first time.

Three years had passed since my trip west with Jake and Will, and in that time I had not been anywhere so surreal as the Salt Flats. Crystal and I parked at the one rest top in the whole expanse and stepped out onto the field of minerals. I once again stood on that vast expanse of white thinking it could easily be mistaken for a snow field if it weren't a hundred degrees out. The two of us stared at the distant mountains wavering in the heat like the mirage of a giant floating island. I was just as enthralled by the landscape this time around, though the experience was soured a bit as we didn't have an air conditioned car to escape to.

Indeed, after replacing the reservoir and refilling the coolant, we were still frequently overheating. Even the suggestion of blowing cold air could lead to another breakdown. We made it through Utah decently, but Nevada... My God, Nevada. Never in heaven nor hell has a demon wrought a land with such fury as Nevada. Hours upon hours of scorching terrain. Every time we crested a hill I worried we were about to crack the radiator. When we couldn't bear the heat any longer we would turn on the AC, but sometimes we'd get no more than twenty seconds of relief before we'd have to switch it off to save the engine. This persisted the entire way from the Utah border to Reno. Drivers may go hundreds of miles across that great expanse without passing any services. A complete meltdown along there would have been more dangerous than I cared to admit.

We were a few miles outside of Reno when the trip odometer rolled over to 1,000 miles. I would watch that happen twice more before the trip was over. Evening was approaching, so we stopped for dinner and to find a shot glass for Crystal's collection. We ate at a diner that was wholly unremarkable. I was nostalgic for the time I'd spent at the National Bowling Stadium with Will and Jake, so I suggested she look for a shot glass there and Crystal obliged. After we found one we hiked up into the stands and watched a few frames of a women's tournament. There were some good bowlers and some not so good ones, but it was fun all the same.

Before long it was time to move on. The sun was starting to set and cooler weather was blowing in, which helped mitigate the overheating problem. We backtracked along I-80 a bit then headed north on US-395. We got to the tree covered in shoes right at sundown and took some pictures. Somehow I didn't think to look for the spot I had signed my initials with Jake and Will during our last trip.

We continued onward to Redding through national forests that we couldn't see in the night. I had driven through them during the day, so I knew they were beautiful, but out there all alone at night... that was something special. We pulled off for fifteen minutes to gaze at the heavens. We couldn't begin to count all the stars overhead. We had a long way to go before we slept though, so we pressed on. We were sixteen miles outside of Redding when the Check Engine light came on.

In that moment I was certain this wasn't going to be one of those stories that we would look back on and laugh, saying, "Boy, it was tough, but we sure had fun." No, this was going to be the opening argument of my insanity plea once I burned my car to the ground in Redding's town square.

Okay, I didn't do anything so drastic. We were held up in Redding until about 3:00 PM the next day though. When we woke to find the Check Engine light still on, we knew we had to talk to a mechanic. I found a place and we managed to get the car in to be looked at that day. After we dropped it off we decided to see what Redding had to offer. We sprawled out in a grassy field for a bit, then shuffled on when the heat started to get to us. We discovered an adorable animal crossing sign a couple blocks away. Apparently a mother duck and her ducklings crossed that street so frequently that they felt the need to warn drivers about it. We sadly did not find the duck family that inspired such a sign.

We stumbled across a restaurant called Lumberjacks with the tagline, "Where the big boys eat!" It made me regret having eaten breakfast at the hotel. We got a table nonetheless and had some ice tea and hash browns and generally loafed about. We had come for the AC, but we stayed for the entertainment. There were maybe a dozen TVs throughout the restaurant, and every single one of them was tuned to re-runs of the Lumberjack World Championships. Canada often kicked ass, but America had some good showings as well. The Swiss team were the underdogs that the producers kept focusing on. It was heart wrenching to see them get knocked out in the semi-finals.

We were especially enamored with the springboard chop. For the uninitiated, here's what that looks like. Say there was a tree that needs to be chopped down. But say, for whatever lumberjack reason, it couldn't be chopped down at the base. Instead it needed to be attacked twelve feet up. What could be done? Apparently the answer was to cut a knock four feet up, shove a surfboard into it, climb onto said surfboard, and repeat the process. We watched a dozen men each ascend a tree in this manner as they raced to be the first to lob off the very top. Seeing them balance precariously on boards as they hacked away with axes was nothing short of glorious.

Around noon we headed back to the mechanic to check the status of our car only to learn they hadn't looked at it yet. I couldn't complain as we had just called for an appointment that morning, so we whiled away the afternoon around the shop. We occasionally chatted and occasionally napped. Eventually they brought my car into the bay. It turned out the Check Engine light was about something that wouldn't affect performance but would take a whole day to fix, so we let it be. They changed the oil because I had sorely miscalculated how many miles this trip would take. They couldn't find any problems with the cooling system, which meant we continued to be perplexed by the engine overheating as we made tracks northwest.

We had to pull off twice to let the car cool down while crossing the mountains from Redding to Crescent City. My car had taken up a new habit of belching coolant all over the side of the road when we stopped, but we had the foresight to buy extra so we could refill whatever we lost. While we were pulled over the first time a surveyor who was working in the area asked if we needed help. I explained the situation to him and told him we'd be fine, so he went about his business. We were back on the road shortly thereafter, then pulled over again within a few miles. As we were once again waiting for the car to cool down, a truck pulled up behind us and turned out to be the same surveyor from before. This time he just laughed and asked if we were sure we were fine. I assured him we were and that was the last we saw of him. As luck would have it, the last summit was just past a couple more bends in the road. From there we coasted down to the ocean without incident.

Finally seeing the Pacific did a hell of a lot to raise our spirits. It wasn't long before we were driving through the mighty redwood forests. Will, Jake, and I had eschewed the chance to see them during our previous trip, so this was a brand new experience for both Crystal and I. We could hardly believe such monumental trees were real. Crystal recorded a video as we passed, but we decided not to stop because the sun was already nearing the horizon. We pulled into Crescent City at a reasonable hour, ate dinner at a seafood restaurant that was decent, and turned in for the night.

We headed north out of Crescent City the next day. We had considered backtracking south to see the redwoods again, but we figured there would be more ahead. Our hunch was correct as we were confronted with even more massive redwoods just a few miles outside of town. We did the touristy thing of pulling over as soon as we saw the first tree. We took pictures and generally marveled at it for a good twenty minutes before hitting the road again. Within five minutes we stopped again because the trees were more enormous still. That time we happened to pull over next to a trailhead, so we hiked around the area for an hour or so. There were actually three trails, two of which were less than a mile and the third was close to four miles. We took the two trails that were less than a mile and ambled up the third a bit before turning back. Not even a hundred yards into the first trail we found a giant redwood that had been felled by lightning. The inside of it was entirely hollow and charred, so Crystal and I had great fun crawling through it like a tunnel.

The rest of the driving that day was rather uneventful. No pulling off due to overheating, just some pleasant stops as we made our way through the last bit of California and on into Oregon. It was early evening when we arrived at Aaron's place in Eugene and met up with him and Sakka. Aaron had just graduated the day before and Sakka had arrived in time to see the ceremony. Aaron's dad had also come to town for the festivities, and he took us to dinner soon after our arrival. Afterward us kids headed over to a local ice cream shop then returned to Aaron's apartment for a night of catching up and generally joking around.

The next morning, all of us able-bodied youngsters got roped into helping Aaron move. His degree was in marine biology, but he needed an additional certification to follow his dream of building exhibits in professional aquariums. That would require another year of study up in Newport. We loaded most of his worldly belongings in a U-Haul and drove it two hours north to a storage locker near his future college. He would be spending the summer at his parents' home in Denver before returning to Oregon in the fall to collect his things and begin class. Once everything was secured we made a beeline for Rogue brewery to have lunch and drinks. The food hit the spot after our labors. Everything was made using their beers, including the specialty ketchup and mustard for my brat. Crystal picked up another shot glass for her collection. This one had the Rogue logo above the tagline, "So you want a revolution?" While chatting up the gift shop clerk we learned that Oregon had recently passed a law allowing all breweries to also distill hard alcohol, so we sauntered over to the brand new Rogue distillery to taste some nice rums and whiskeys. I ended up buying a bottle of their single malt and Crystal grabbed a bottle of their Hazelnut Rum.

After Aaron's dad left to return the U-Haul we decided to check out a kitschy little tourist trap nearby. We took photos under a plaster shark head styled to look like it was bursting through a wall to chomp on our heads. We wandered into a little rock shop that wasn't half bad, and the lady running it was very nice. She gave us a tip on a beach nearby where bald eagles had been roosting lately. We headed there and had a nice walk, albeit lacking in bald eagle sightings, before heading back to Eugene. We ate dinner at a pizza shop near Aaron's apartment then whiled away the evening watching videos on YouTube.

We made plans to grab breakfast the next morning at a little joint near campus. It was an alright place and every table had a little IQ Test game where the player jumped pegs on a triangle grid to remove other pegs. In general, the fewer the pegs left when no more moves could be made the better the score. Three was pretty good, two was awesome, one was incredible, though the mother lode of points actually came if the player left eight of the fourteen pegs on the board with no moves remaining. It struck me as an interesting way to approach the problem.

Crystal bought breakfast as a graduation present to Sakka and Aaron, then we headed to a local bookstore of interest. It was there that we said our goodbyes to Aaron and his dad. They had another load to run to Newport and needed to hit the road. We perused the store for a while. Sakka bought seven books in the time it took me to find one, but I would have been happy to simply spend time in a bookstore even if I hadn't found anything.

With our shopping done, it was finally time for the three of us to set off. We took I-5 north out of Eugene for the second time in twenty-four hours and had another uneventful drive up to Seattle. I was hopeful that our overheating woes were behind us.

We found our way to Dianne's house and got a tour of her domain. She lived in a collection of townhouses situated on a pretty steep hill. When I say steep hill I mean if we walked out her front door we could easily step up onto the roof of the two-story bike shop that neighbored her complex. Of course that's what we did, primarily because Dianne had three dozen plants and two beehives on their roof. Dianne informed us when we arrived that she was overdue for checking if the queen in each hive was still alive, so she and Crystal donned beekeeper outfits and began deconstructing the plywood apiaries. Sakka and I stood and watched from the sidelines. Dianne explained the peculiarities of bee behavior as she worked. First and foremost, bees tend to fly in a straight line away from the hive entrance. That meant that when she initially constructed the boxes with the opening pointing at her home, she had in essence created a cannon that shot live bees at her building all day long. She knew something had to be done when complaints started rolling in, but that's also when she learned that bees are easily confused by any change to the hive. Even rotating it too abruptly could leave the bees unable to find their way inside. Thus began a week long process of gradually adjusting the apiaries until they pointed safely away from the townhouses.

Once we were done inspecting the hives we made a dinner of salmon, potatoes, and a spear grass as Dianne so colorfully deemed it. It was quite nice, though I did call shenanigans on Sakka. Any time I tried to help with dinner prep or cooking Sakka would chase me out of the kitchen with a dismissive, "There's nothing for you here." As soon as we finished eating though, who else but Sakka suggested the person that didn't help with dinner should do all the dishes? Make no mistake, that was all part of her master plan. Regardless, I relegated myself to the wash basin. After all that was behind us we played a brief game of Trivial Pursuit, more accurately Children's Trivial Pursuit, and turned in for the night.

At breakfast Dianne noticed a bandage on my finger and inquired as to my injury. I informed her that it was to cover a wart so that I didn't spread infection, to which she replied that liquid nitrogen would fix that right up. "Yes," I said, "but where can we find liquid nitrogen at such an hour?" Little did I know that later that day the four of us would be in Dianne's car driving down the streets of Seattle, Crystal and I in the back, and I would have an open container of liquid nitrogen in my lap while I applied it to my hand with a wadded up paper towel.

I say an open container of liquid nitrogen, but that doesn't really do justice to the situation. It likely conjures the image of an OSHA approved liquid nitrogen carrying vessel with a secure, albeit no longer factory sealed, lid. No. No no no. What I had equated to roughly a soup bowl half filled with bubbling liquid nitrogen in my lap, and the streets of Seattle did not make for a smooth track. There were hills and sharp turns and bumps and potholes. Had I ever wondered what it was like to splash liquid nitrogen on my crotch, I would soon learn that *it's not very fun*.

Allow me to back up a bit as plenty happened between breakfast and my escapade with the liquid nitrogen. It was drizzling that morning, but we knew we had to venture forth and see the city proper. We hopped the bus downtown and saw the Space Needle on our way, which was painted orange at the time. Dianne informed us that it was originally orange and for the 50th anniversary they repeated history. Maybe some old Seattleites could reminisce about it being orange, but it looked like a fried egg to us. We thought about going to the top of it, but we decided the cost was too exorbitant. Instead we opted for the Sky View Observatory at the Columbia Center where we took pictures of ourselves literally looking down our noses at the Space Needle. A nearby sign pointed out the Olympic Mountains, but Seattle weather being what it was we had to take that on faith.

The next stop was the Seattle Public Library, which was a fantastic piece of architecture. The floors wound together in a great spiral so the entire library was accessible without setting foot on any stairs. We took the escalator to the tenth floor and began a walking descent. The library's stacks began at the top and extended down to the sixth floor. It wasn't long before

Sakka and Dianne decided to take the elevator back to the ground floor. Crystal and I wanted to experience the library in all its glory, so we ambled down the full height of it. I've always found something enchanting about wandering through a library or even just a bookstore. To walk down the vast rows of publications is to feel the immense weight of the collective human knowledge pressing upon my being. Picking up a book is the tactile experience of abstract thought. It's a connection to the whole of human knowledge, and I was happy to immerse myself in it that day.

We met up with Dianne and Sakka back on the ground floor and then proceeded to Pike's Place Market, world renowned for their mongers that literally throw fish back and forth to one another. When we arrived there were a few dozen people milling about, cameras at the ready, acting as though a fish could be thrown at any moment. For their own part, the fishmongers were doing menial tasks about the shop because they had a business to run and didn't throw their product around for the hell of it. Determined not to be slack jawed tourists like the rest of the crowd, we quickly set our sights elsewhere. Of course, as soon as we turned our backs we heard a commotion as an actual customer placed an order for sockeye and the fish began to fly. Our moral high ground did not make for a good vantage point, so we missed the whole thing. We went around the corner to Pike's Place Chowder where we consoled ourselves with bowls of the best chowder I've had in my life.

The day was quickly getting away from us, and Dianne had an errand to attend to before it got too late. She was doing research at the university as part of her degree and needed to check on a school of zebrafish that formed the basis of her work. We followed her through the labyrinthine hallways to a laboratory that housed shelves upon shelves of small plastic bins with fish inside. She explained her work to us, then gave us a tour of the building. One room had a heavily insulated container of liquid nitrogen available for use by any of the university researchers. There were no heavily insulated travel vessels though. Instead Dianne produced the cereal bowl I mentioned earlier, filled it up, and handed it to me for the purpose of freezing my wart. Thus began our unnerving drive back to Dianne's neighborhood.

We stopped for dinner at a little Italian place that put butcher paper down on the tables. Dianne drew an elaborate orca on it that was sectioned into different images of classic Seattle landmarks. We could only hope that it made its way into some Doodle of Fame binder. After dinner we met up with Dianne's boyfriend Ken and a group of their friends for some board games. While we were playing someone knocked on the front door and tried to swindle Ken out of ten dollars. There was a common scam in Seattle where someone would knock on the door and give an elaborate story about being locked out and needing money to pay the locksmith. Another guy had tried it on Dianne a couple weeks before. The story made absolutely no sense and Ken was having none of it, so he sent the guy packing.

We left Seattle the next morning heading east. We hit I-90 and made good time in spite of nearly overheating multiple times as we traversed the Cascades. Eastern Washington was a little easier going, which was nice as the terrain out there was not conducive to hanging around a broken down car. Lush deciduous forests had given way to sweltering shrub lands. The landscape felt strangely similar to the dusty plains of eastern Colorado. I never would have guessed if I hadn't seen it with my own eyes.

Fortunately we didn't have far to go that day. Sakka was itching to see her uncle and cousins in Spokane, and we were happy to oblige. The evening was spent visiting with them and included a dinner of salmon, potatoes, and asparagus once more. I spent most of my time playing with the family dog. I could have sworn she was about two years old with how spryly she chased the ball around the backyard, but I later learned she was thirteen. Some dogs never grow up I suppose. Crystal and I bunked in cousin Leah's room and marveled at her collectables. The highlights included a sealed, collector's edition Star Trek PEZ set and a scale model of the Batmobile from the Adam West TV show.

The sun was barely up as we were saying our goodbyes the following morning. We took off at 6:00 AM anticipating a sixteen hour drive to put us in Denver around 10:00 PM. Continued engine trouble would cause that to grow into a twenty hour drive with us arriving around 2:00 AM. Crystal found a shot glass shaped like a potato shortly after entering Idaho that was an obvious choice for her collection. The day was mercifully overcast until we got to Montana. Apparently clouds could not contain the Big Sky state. Somehow it was worse than crossing Nevada as evidenced by how many times we needed to pull off and let the engine cool down. Sharp rises in elevation were a guaranteed breakdown, but even gradual inclines took a toll. At least once we pulled over just as the highway began sloping up, waited ten minutes for the engine to cool down, set off, and overheated again before the road had a chance to level out.

The time we spent on the side of the road eventually became a much needed break. There was no possibility of using the AC while we drove, so we had to choose between blasting across the countryside with the windows open or sweating through the stagnant heat with the windows up. Rolling them down seemed like the obvious choice in spite of the deafening roar of the wind through the car. In reality though, the air outside felt like hot breath pouring over our faces any time we tried it. Thus we spent most of the drive with the windows up. Crystal and I had become somewhat numb to the torment by that day, but this was the worst Sakka had it that trip. She spent hours that day trying to nap as a mental escape from the heat. It made my heart ache a little every time I looked in the rear view mirror and saw her sweltering in the backseat.

The sun was starting to set as we entered Wyoming, but that didn't give us any respite from the heat. Our prayers for lower temperatures wouldn't be answered until we hit a tremendous thunderstorm as we passed Cheyenne on the last leg of our trip. For the time being we pulled off in Sheridan to get some food and wait for the temperature to drop a few degrees. Over dinner we found out from Sakka that her mom was actually born and raised there. Seeing as we were already hours behind on our journey we didn't have the time to explore the town, which was a damn shame. Sakka always wanted to spend some actual time there. All of her relatives moved out of Sheridan long before she arrived on the scene, so she never had a reason to stop there on her family vacations up north.

I hope she's made that trip in the intervening years. A place could be as much a piece of a family as the actual people, and family meant a lot to Sakka. We didn't spend the night in Spokane because it was convenient. We could have split the drive from Seattle to Denver more evenly and saved ourselves one of the most brutal days of driving I've ever experienced. That would have meant missing the chance to spend an evening with Sakka's uncle and cousins though, and we wouldn't have traded that for anything else.

Afterword

Admittedly, I didn't promise you much at the beginning of this book. I promised a collection of my stories, and I suppose at this point I can say I've delivered. I've spent the past five years compiling them in coffee shops, hotel rooms, airports, bus stations, hospitals, universities, and anywhere else I could get a wifi signal. Some were transcribed from old journal entries, others were lifted from emails among friends, and still others were written from memory alone. So, why did I put them all in a book? There has to be some deeper meaning here, right? What's the point of all this?

The way I figure it, everyone has a lifetime of their own stories. There are countless tales to be told and even more being made every minute of every day. Those stories mean something, even if only to the person experiencing them. They matter. And one of two things can happen to them:

they can die with us, or they can be told and live on. If those are the only two options then why wouldn't we share them?

Still though, why did I choose to write *these* stories? What makes them so important to me? Well, to answer that, let me tell you one more:

This story takes place in 2012, during my grueling trip to the Pacific Northwest with Crystal. We had just overheated for the first time while crossing Wyoming along I-80. Crystal was on the phone with Uncle Seb to decide if we could fix the car once we got to Ogden; I was scouring the area for scrap wood that I could use to pry the cap off the scalding hot coolant system. Just then, as we were suffering the worst setback of any of our trips together, we were engulfed by a swarm of butterflies. We couldn't believe it. Way out in the sticks, with nothing but withering grass as far as the eye could see, we were engulfed by butterflies.

That was the most difficult trip I have ever taken. If Crystal hadn't been there to see me through I probably would have given up at the first sign of trouble in Wyoming, but together we salvaged it and even managed to have some incredible moments. Such was the way with Crystal. As long as I'd known her she had a determined air about her that saw us through countless mishaps on the road, from our breakdowns across the Northwest to our mad dash toward New England. She also had the humor to laugh at every tough situation. Because of that we will always have the butterflies.

That's why I chose these stories. They are the roots that have kept me connected to so many amazing people for decades. I lied to you in the beginning, these are not my stories.

These are our stories. Over the course of a decade of travel I found the people that could lead me to places I never imagined. The people that enabled me to be who I truly am. The people who always stood by me and who I would gladly stand by as well. The people that sought wonder in everything they did. The people that taught me about the world beyond my backyard. The people that could see a terrible situation and run headlong toward it rather than cower from it. The people that valued relationships above everything else.

If you can do the same then all that's left is to chase your own butterflies.

About the Author

Nathan Thompson grew up in Boulder, Colorado, where he attended college at the University of Colorado. He graduated in 2011 with a Bachelor of Arts in English Literature and a Bachelor of Science in Computer Science. After years of working as a software engineer, he combined his passions and founded asdf Publishing with a commitment to support and advance technological innovation in the field of literature. Nathan now lives in Lafayette, Colorado, with his wife, daughter, and Bernese Mountain Dog.